D664396

D0997066

Vision Critical Studies

General Editor: Michael Egan

Margaret Drabble:
Puritanism and Permissiveness

Vision Critical Studies published and in preparation:

Henry James: The Ibsen Years

E. E. Cummings: A Remembrance of Miracles

The Silent Majority: A Study of the Working Class in Post-war British Fiction

Wyndham Lewis: Fictions and Satires

The Fiction of Sex: Themes and Functions of Sex Difference in the Twentieth-century Novel

George Gissing

Historical Novel and Popular Politics in Nineteenth-century England

The Plays of D. H. Lawrence

Reaching into the Silence: A Study of Eight Twentieth-century Visionaries

MARGARET DRABBLE:
PURITANISM AND
PERMISSIVENESS

Valerie Grosvenor Myer

VISION

Vision Press Limited
157 Knightsbridge
London, SW1X 7PA

ISBN 0 85478 063 7

**To Michael
who made it all happen**

Printed in Great Britain
by Clarke, Doble & Brendon Ltd
Plymouth
MCMLXXIV

Contents

5

Editorial Note

Vision Critical Studies will examine mainly nineteenth century and contemporary imaginative writing, delimiting an area of literary inquiry between, on the one hand, the loose generalities of the "readers' guide" approach and, on the other, the excessively particular specialist study. Crisply written and with an emphasis on fresh insights, the series will gather its coherence and direction from a broad congruity of approach on the part of its contributors. Each volume, based on sound scholarship and research, but relatively free from cumbersome scholarly apparatus, will be of interest and value to all students of the period.

M.E.E.

Acknowledgements

My thanks are due to Alison and David McRobb for valuable suggestions incorporated into Chapter 7. Any errors are my own.

My thanks are also due to the following publishers for permission to quote from the works listed: Allen & Unwin (*The Protestant Ethic and the Spirit of Capitalism*, by Max Weber, 1930); MacGibbon & Kee (*Leslie Stephen: A Biography*, by Noel Annan, 1951); John Murray (*Religion and the Rise of Capitalism*, by R. H. Tawney, 1926); Oxford University Press, New York (*For Max Weber: Essays in Sociology* pub. Routledge & Kegan Paul, 1948); and to Weidenfeld & Nicolson (*Early Victorians 1832–1851*, by J. F. C. Harrison, 1971) and from the works of Margaret Drabble. In the United States, to William Morrow, Inc., for the works of Margaret Drabble; Harcourt Brace Jovanovich (*Religion and the Rise of Capitalism*, by R. H. Tawney); Gollancz (*The Puritan Pleasures of the Detective Story from Sherlock Holmes to Van der Valk*, by Eric Routley, 1972); Yale University Press (*The Victorian Frame of Mind*, by Walter E. Houghton, 1957); and to Macmillan (*Collected Poems of W. B. Yeats*, 1933).

PART ONE

The Reluctant Puritan

1

Success and failure

Margaret Drabble is the most contemporary of novelists: a whole generation of women readers identifies with her characters, who they feel represent their own problems. Her heroines were preoccupied with the difficulties of fulfilment and self-definition in a man's world, the conflicting claims of selfhood, wifehood and motherhood, long before the women's lib movement really got going.

Most of her leading characters are women, attractive and highly educated. In youth they are bewildered by their twin destiny, as intelligentsia on the one hand and as sexual beings on the other. How to reconcile the two? Drabble heroines suffer characteristically from a combination of intellectual arrogance and diffidence, a fear of their gifts and confusion as to how they should be used.

Early in life, characters have vast longings and, despite their puzzlement, enormous bright expectations. These expectations are rarely fulfilled: they find themselves trapped in marriage, with its routines of housework, breastfeeding, nappies, taking the children to the park and perambulators in the hall.

This contrast between expectation and experience has been shared by a generation of educated women and has been endlessly discussed since Judith Hubback wrote *Wives Who Went to College*. Graduate wives are, of course, a minority by reason of their privileges, but there are enough of them to see their problems reflected in Margaret Drabble's heroines, most of whom are unhappy. This is not to imply that all educated housewives and mothers are discontented: but such discontent has become fashionable.

Margaret Drabble's contribution to our understanding of the contemporary social scene is based on the situation of the "graduate wife" but goes much further. The area she has made her own is that of motherhood: pregnancy, birth, lactation and maternal care. Mothers respond to Margaret Drabble's accounts of mother-love with delighted recognition: "That's just how it is." Most previous women novelists have been childless. Penelope Mortimer's treatment of motherhood in *The Pumpkin Eater* is less about the narrator's own maternal urges than their effects upon the second husband. Motherhood is a central experience in the life of Margaret Drabble's characters and maternal love a means to salvation.

Characteristically her heroines resent their pregnancies, but are overwhelmed with love when the children are born. They find it harder to live in peace and love with the fathers (see Chapter 6). Although she finds many male readers, Margaret Drabble is a "woman's novelist" in that she reflects primarily (but not exclusively) female concerns and female conflicts. An exception to this is the impressive characterisation of Simon in *The Needle's Eye* (see Chapters 3, 4 and 11).

If graduate wives were all she was writing about, she would be of merely historical interest, reflecting a minor social crisis of our time. She is a popular novelist in the best sense, but her popularity has worked against due recognition of her art. Her novels show a progression from self-centred heroines and their adjustment problems to a wider probing of the basis of relationships in society. In *The Needle's Eye* she offers an extended analysis of the nature of social relationships, the relations between love and money. Her books are more than variations on the theme of the graduate wife chained to a bucket of wet nappies: her leading characters are all intelligent and articulate and all have problems, but they are sharply differentiated and used to explore moral issues of increasing complexity.

Salvation is what every leading character is looking for (see Chapter 7). Margaret Drabble told a church full of people during a lunchtime dialogue at St Mary-le-Bow, Cheapside, on September 12, 1972, that she "felt the need for God, but could not be sure he was there." She added, "I have more confidence in myself as a mother than in Him as a Father." She might have been speaking for most of her heroines in this. For her, the best hope for humanity lies in human love.

Whether or not God is there, moral decisions remain. Margaret Drabble's continuing theme is a reconsideration and revaluation of the English puritan tradition. She has recognised that this strain, though popularly denied, is still very much with us and has left us an inheritance of guilt and anxiety. This perception has enabled her to portray with sympathy, accuracy and sharpness those classes of English society where the puritan tradition is strongest: "liberal" intellectuals and the northern lower middle class. She understands these social areas and writes with perceptive insight about the influence of early conditioning (see Chapter 4). Her characteristic strengths are accurate social observation, epigrammatic wit, compassion and a coherent metaphysic (see Chapter 7).

The extended analysis of the puritan inheritance, played out in all her leading characters, is her characteristic and unique contribution to the contemporary novel. Rosamund in *The Mill-stone* says, "This morality is my own whether I like it or not." The size of the Drabble readership suggests that many readers recognise it as theirs as well.

In Rosamund's case her inherited morality is in some ways a source of strength: in the case of Clara's parents (*Jerusalem the Golden*) and Simon's mother (*The Needle's Eye*) puritanism is shown at its least appealing, manifested in meanness, spiritual and financial, and the denial of love.

Clara and Simon have to fight their way upwards in society, and Margaret Drabble treats sympathetically and with conviction the conflicts and tensions imposed by their social mobility. She recognises and portrays the cost of the educational climb: Clara is painfully fulfilling her own nature in making it, Simon, bowing to his mother's will, is distorting his. The problem for her characters is how to fulfil the demands of their own natures without violating conscience.

"Intellectualism, moralism and the . . . values of the city" are seen by Dr Erik Routley (*The Puritan Pleasures of the Detective Story from Sherlock Holmes to Van der Valk*) as "the positive principle in the English puritan tradition." This definition is necessarily partial and inadequate, as the terms are undefined in their context. Any definition of the complex of attitudes known collectively as puritanism is open to objection. Nevertheless, certain forms of moral scrupulosity, even rigidity, an intellectual interest in moral questions, anxiety about salvation, the social virtues of thrift, hard work, self-denial and effort, are generally and popularly recognised as "puritanical." Whether puritanism implies "the values of the city" is a more difficult question, raising issues outside the scope of my enquiry, such as the influence of Arnold's "Philistines," the nineteenth-century mercantile classes.

But the words "puritanism" and "puritanical" are recurrent in Margaret Drabble's books, and Dr Routley's formulation strikingly fits her leading characters.

Drabble characters all live in London (except for Emma's brief exile in *The Garrick Year*, which precipitates her moral crisis), all are highly intelligent and conscious of it—most of them are Oxbridge graduates—and they all have active, anxious consciences (see Chapter 3), whether they deny or obey their inner moral commands.

Characters ponder their destinies, speculate on metaphysical questions, and try to work out what is right and what is wrong in an allegedly permissive society. In the last couple of years, there has been a growing recognition that "permissiveness" is not such a simple concept as it may once have seemed, and that society now is not so permissive as some have imagined. Margaret Drabble grasped and explored these truths before they became fashionable currency.

Drabble characters, because of their puritan inheritance, equate permissiveness with decadence. Emma in *The Garrick Year* ponders what she sees as "our tatty sexual decadence"; Clara in *Jerusalem the Golden* recognises that her self-propelled rise to education and middle-class culture could be seen as "decadent" because of its ruthlessness; Jane in *The Waterfall* is never sure whether the adulterous love she sees fitfully as her "salvation" is actually "decadent" and "corrupt." Most of the heroines are working towards some kind of clarification, some degree of reconciliation between the demands of their instinctive natures and the moralistic puritan conscience. As Margaret Drabble matures as a writer, this reconciliation becomes harder for her created characters. In the fifth and sixth books there comes the recognition that such reconciliation can only be partial.

But experience is to some extent clarified for the characters and a set of values which will enable them to survive is implied. These values (except in *Jerusalem the Golden*, which falls outside Margaret Drabble's characteristic pattern and is morally open-ended) turn out to be the puritan ones of duty, responsibility (particularly for children) and even renunciation—though grand gestures of renunciation, in the sixth novel, *The Needle's Eye*, are shown not to be enough. What is demanded by life are the smaller renunciations dictated by social responsibility.

The world is bleak: there is no escaping the presence of evil, chance events can be propitious or disastrous, we are predestined to a certain extent by heredity and the grip of environment, laws of necessity and moral causation rule. Having made our beds we must lie on them and everything must be paid for. The Spanish proverb, "Take what you want, said God, take it and pay for it," underlies Margaret Drabble's work.

But we have free will to make our moral choices and there is always the possibility of enlightenment and renewal through grace, when love comes into our hearts. The stern puritan virtues must be softened by love, by fellow-feeling, by community. The ability to love can come only from reconciliation with the demands of one's own nature. "Nature" is used in Margaret Drabble's work with a multiplicity of meanings, and is imaged chiefly by vegetation. Human beings who learn to love will survive, like small hardy plants.

In her work as a whole, the puritan ethic, with its virtues of thrift, self-denial and hard work, is respected but only partially vindicated. In two of her characters, Jane in *The Waterfall* and Rose in *The Needle's Eye*, self-denial and excessive thrift are symptoms of mental disturbance. The puritan virtues are only justified when they serve a useful purpose in making other people happy. When they become self-punishing, they are pointless and destructive, and distort the personality, taking it away from its true goal, harmony with nature.

This central message emerges from all her novels. It gives her work as a whole coherence and development, though some of the novels are more successful in dramatising this issue than others.

Although the characters intellectually reject the puritan inheritance (analysed in Chapters 2 to 7) they are nevertheless conditioned by it. The author is in like case, and this tension provides her main subject matter, the search for values.

Artistically, too, her successes and failures are bound up with this tension. Intellectually she implies that the moralistic puritan conscience should be transcended by the values of love. Artistically her books are successful when she convinces us that the characters have recognised this necessity, as part of their growth. In her earlier and less successful books, we are merely told that they have done so, but we have not felt them doing it.

In *A Summer Birdcage*, the narrator-heroine, Sarah, wanders about wondering what to do with her first from Oxford, longing for community and her sister's love. Sarah, despite luxurious tastes, is restrained by a puritanical conscience (see Chapter 3). Her sister, who is by contrast amoral, marries for money but ends up with her first love. She turns to Sarah in her marital crisis and Sarah finds some comfort at last in the belief that her sister must love her. The book is sharply observant and entertaining; it reflects accurately the frustrations of one kind of woman graduate who has been unable to follow up her academic success.

But the book isn't really about finding family love, whatever the ending may say. The reconciliation with her sister is only a partial solution to Sarah's problem of fulfilment, and not really related to her discovery that one might as well give up "looking for Dostoevskys in corners" and prefer "a good laugh." The Louise-Stephen-John plot is shadowy; so are all the characters, except the narrator. Sarah has a boyfriend in America, we are told, but she seems to think very little about him. She shows so little awareness of other people's needs that the book's moral solution is weakened. The overriding impression is of the unbearable pressure of her own conflicts, and we are not convinced that they are even partially resolved.

Emma in *The Garrick Year* has similar conflicts. She suffers from housewife's malaise. Emma's values predate those of swinging London by at least two years: she is fascinated by the modern, the "bright, glittering, louche"; she adores eccentric bric-à-brac; she loves excitement. Margaret Drabble has her finger on the current cultural pulse, one of the secrets of her wide appeal. Emma, thwarted in her own ambitions, resents her husband's career, has an affair and is finally, we are told, reconciled to herself and to life.

Emma has, it appears, learned deeper values. Her salvation (which she has previously recognised as lying in small acts of self-sacrifice for her daughter, Flora) comes, apparently, after she has jumped into a flooded river to rescue the child from drowning. There are hints that she has been baptised by her total immersion in the floodwaters and has found rebirth. Stripping naked afterwards, she has become a "poor, bare forked animal" who has shed her sophistications with her clothing.

Flora's danger brings out in Emma a renewal of maternal, human love. After moral doubts about appearing naked to her child and her lover together, she starts worrying about her younger child. If Emma were as "perverse" as she has claimed, as far from salvation, she would enjoy the piquancy of being naked with both her lover (incarnation of her temptation to irresponsibility) and her dependent child. Motherhood and its ties, despite her early hatred of "the filthy mess of pregnancy and birth" are what, we gather, reconcile her to herself. Emma has committed herself to the current by a moment's decision: the same current in which her friend Julian, the victim of indecision, drowns himself.

But then other things happen, and we are no longer sure which incident is responsible for Emma's renewal. The adultery with Wyndham comes later. Emma does not enjoy it, and feels afterwards that she has been punished by a car accident. She discovers that her husband is having an affair with her friend Sophy. It is not quite clear which of her experiences releases her from "ignorance": her discovery of David's adultery, her eventual submission to Wyndham, her conviction of punishment, her act of self-sacrifice or her alignment with Sophy, whom Emma has chosen in preference to the over-civilised Mary.

The link between conventional maternal self-sacrifice and the endorsement of "the natural" in the silly Sophy (whose coat Emma significantly puts on after her dip—see Chapter 9) seems arbitrary, an act of will on the part of the author. Like Rosamund, Margaret Drabble seems here to believe "in instinct, on principle" (see Chapter 6). The writer is herself unsure of the relative weight which should be given to "nature" and to "civilisation," an uncertainty which causes her artistic trouble as we shall see in *Jerusalem the Golden.* The ambivalence about Sophy, with her "bloom, like fruit," her beauty, vulgarity and silliness, betrays the author's hesitation. Margaret Drabble's solution to the problem of reconciling the natural and the civilised is to look to the arts (see Chapter 8). But even here, as we see from the imagery (see Chapter 9) of *Jerusalem the Golden,* she is not sure under which heading the arts should come.

To return to *The Garrick Year*: Emma's conversion, though symbolically underscored by the baptismal image, doesn't altogether happen in terms we can feel and follow, because there are too many incidents and we are not clear as to their significance. Emma, it is suggested, has finally become reconciled to her own instincts, has arrived at self-knowledge and has found her true nature. But this resolution is not clearly dramatised and is even overshadowed by the moralism we are invited to reject: are we to agree with Emma that she has been "punished"? The weight we are supposed to give to the puritan values here is not clarified.

The Millstone, perhaps the most popular of Margaret Drabble's novels (and the only one to be filmed, from her own screenplay) was serialised in *Woman's Mirror* (where Rosamund's Ph.D. research was simplified so that she was merely "writing a book") and on BBC "Woman's Hour" (where editors cut out the vital parts about Rosamund's formative background). Women all over Britain identified with this brave, sympathetic unmarried mother, courageously bearing her burden alone. Gillian Tindall has accused Margaret Drabble of sentimentalising Rosamund and of displaying in this book "a mean female chauvinism." Neither of these interpretations does justice to the scope of the book or reflects the truth about it, as I hope to show.

Rosamund stigmatises herself as a freak: our judgement is less harsh, and qualified by sympathy. But she is, like Emma (and with more inner consistency), a most unusual and individual woman, yet representative of the currents of our time. She is in many ways quite extraordinary, yet we believe in her, because of the accumulation of imaginative, truthful sociological and psychological detail. There is real insight in the characterisation.

The use of first-person narration in this book is brilliant, bettered in Drabble's work only by that of Jane in *The Waterfall.*

Rosamund reveals to us, without stepping for one moment out of character, her strengths and weaknesses, reminisces about the upbringing which has so strongly conditioned her (see Chapter 4). The experience of unmarried motherhood brings her out of her ivory tower of scholarship: her attitudes to both aspects of her life are dramatised with truth and understanding (see Chapters 4, 6 and 8). She instinctively loves her baby, but cannot extend her new-found capacity for loving to anybody else, not even the baby's father. Rosamund is ultimately judged and placed for us: her puritan nonconformist conscience, of which she is explicitly and acutely aware, gives her paradoxical sources of strength, but limits her full human development. Here, characterisation (searching, delicately precise and powerful) is at one with plot and the integral abstract ideas as it was not in *The Garrick Year* or *A Summer Birdcage*. Rosamund never achieves full maturity, but with her creation Margaret Drabble arrives at maturity as a writer. *The Millstone* is her first coherent artistic success. In it she successfully exploits her central interests. Rosamund is an unhappy graduate mother, fighting in isolation the residual puritanism she would like to reject but cannot.

Jerusalem the Golden shows a broadening of social range, an extension of sympathies and a change of direction. The heroine is no longer a refined Oxbridge graduate from a privileged, comfortable background, but a lower middle-class climber. Previous Drabble heroines have been, in background and circumstances, nearer to herself: here she takes a successful imaginative leap into the mind of a very different kind of educated woman. The social observation in this book is so brilliantly accurate, the touch so sure, that the impression is one of satirical wit. But careful reading shows a sympathetic understanding of Clara's plight. "She had affection in her and nowhere to spend it." She is not a likeable heroine, as the previous ones, despite their quirks, are; she shares their toughness, but lacks their moral scruples.

Although *Jerusalem the Golden* shows a growth in stature, moving in directions which are later developed in *The Needle's Eye* with more surety, certain problems remain unresolved. The treatment of the Denham family as a whole is uneasy. (For analysis of this uneasiness in terms of imagery, see Chapter 10). An obvious flaw is that we get so little of Clelia Denham's

21

allegedly brilliant conversation, although we are shown her moral qualities in action: her generosity, her maternal care for somebody else's baby, her concern for and interest in other people. Her brother Gabriel, even less strongly characterised, has (we are told) a puzzling "strict inheritance," though there is nothing in his family background to account for it. He is seen acting in accordance with this strictness in staying faithful to his impossible, neurotic wife. But it is never otherwise explained or established, so the information that his affair with Clara brings him "incipient gaiety" loses its potential dramatic force. Uncharacteristically, too, *Jerusalem the Golden* is morally less conclusive than the other books: we are left with the open-ended situation that Clara is involved with the Denham family largely through an affair with an unhappily married man. Whether their conduct is to be regarded as right or wrong, there is no indication. Such things happen, the author seems to be saying, and leaving it at that. (A more profound moral judgement on a similar situation comes in her next book, *The Waterfall*, where Margaret Drabble reverts to her earlier style of subject matter, a lonely graduate wife, though Jane is in fact the only heroine who is both married and a graduate.)

The content of *Jerusalem the Golden* is not sexual morality, but social change. The point seems to be that the days of hereditary privilege are over and the heirs will be first-generation upstarts from the universities like Clara, a mournful but inevitable process. But it is hard to see why Margaret Drabble should choose to show inherited wealth and culture as in incipient decay. The "limitless vistas" Clara finds in the Denham house and garden are limited for us by the dying flowers in the house, the weeds in their garden, and the failures of the Denham children in adult life which they symbolise. There is no observable sociological reason for this: the children of the gifted are often successful.

The true energy in the book is Clara's, and Clara is greedy and destructive, though she eventually wins through to seeing the possibility of love. For her, the Denhams represent perfection. Margaret Drabble clearly admires them too, then weights the scales against them. For Clara, escape from the negative aspects of puritanism is a driving force: she must grow by "will and strain." This effort can involve distortion, but when the necessity for effort is removed, as it is with the comfortable Denham children, decadence sets in. Margaret Drabble would like to endorse the Denham world, full of art and love, but she betrays her own doubts about a way of life from which all puritan restraints have been removed. These doubts conflict with the omniscient authorial statements about the values celebrated in the Denhams; it is unlikely that the narration here represents merely Clara's perceptions. The author's ambivalence is disturbing rather than suggestive: her partial rejection seems unnecessarily severe, an expression of the puritanism she intellectually condemns.

Clara goes after what she wants single-mindedly. Jane, narrator of *The Waterfall*, is literally in two minds. Her characterisation is another triumph. Jane is driven into a schizoid state by her experiences (although she later claims, unconvincingly, to have been sane all the time) and the story of her adulterous affair is narrated alternately in the third person (Freudian superego) and the first (id). She fails to reconcile the two, contradicts herself, but like Yeats's Crazy Jane discovers some paradoxical truths about life and love.

Margaret Drabble said in an interview with John Horder in *The Times*:

> It was about the painfully depressive side I wanted to write . .
> the side that can hardly cope with any aspect of living . . . I was
> thereby able to confront my own worst fears. . . . My heroines
> have all been competent women, full of practical common sense.
> I wanted to write about a very different sort of woman . . . I
> can't bear doing nothing; and this is why I have tried to face
> the pathological state of inactivity in *The Waterfall*. Also the fear
> of complete abandonment which sometimes goes hand in glove
> with extreme passivity.

Jane's description of herself as "schizoid" is beautifully dramatised in her narrative. *The Waterfall* appears at first reading as formless and fluid as the mind of its narrator. This apparent shapelessness is transcended by an art which creates a coherent and beautiful pattern out of incoherence and contradiction. This is achieved by a developing pattern of qualifying statements about what has been said before (see Chapter 8), structural parallels and interlinked patterns of imagery (see Chapter 9).

Jane tries to write an autobiographical novel, but finds her material too complex to fit into neat patterns like the poetry she writes. That the book achieves order out of disorder, reflecting the qualifications and inconclusiveness of life itself, yet conveying an ambiguous truth, is Margaret Drabble's success: it does not belong to Jane. Jane aims at transcendence, but in her own opinion fails:

> It won't, of course, do: as an account, I mean, of what took place . . . don't let me deceive myself, I see no virtue in confusion. I see true virtue in clarity, in consistency, in communication, in honesty.

She fails in simple clarity and consistency. The book remains ambiguous, which makes ultimately for its artistic success, but not in the terms envisaged by its heroine narrator. Jane does not achieve honesty, either with herself or in her relations with Lucy, her cousin and her lover's wife. *The Waterfall* makes painful reading, as Jane's agony of mind is dramatised with needle-sharp accuracy. The final conclusion that sexual love and the mental healing it brings are worth the sacrifice of conventional morality is fought for every inch of the way. At the end, Jane is not even intellectually convinced that the sacrifice was justified, although this is the clear meaning her story has for us. She only knows that her earlier intimation that love must be paid for in suffering was true.

The truth Jane does succeed in communicating is that it is impossible to see the whole truth, let alone tell it, because any individual's vision is necessarily partial. Margaret Drabble said at the lunchtime dialogue in church already mentioned that one of her continuing preoccupations as a writer was the difficulty of telling the truth. We catch Jane out in lies, self-deception, confusion, yet out of the distance between her and us the true pattern emerges. In *A Summer Birdcage* Sarah was not sufficiently distanced for us to see her clearly in relation to the other characters. In *The Waterfall* this narrative balance is perfectly poised.

The Waterfall remains Margaret Drabble's most achieved work of art, but the weakness (as in all her books, except *The Needle's Eye*, more ambitious but over-schematic) is in the male characters. Jane's husband Malcolm, always off-stage, will pass; her lover

James won't quite do. Allowing for the way Jane desperately tries to remake him in her own image (so that a man who loves getting away in fast cars is said at one point to find confinement and solitude suited to his nature, as to hers), we are given nothing to make it likely that he would share her morbid moral values. Yet he is made to say, improbably, that Norway is "a serious place" where they will all "suffer together." If she has influenced his ways of thinking, there is no other evidence of it. He tells her, rightly, that she is mad. James is not a character we can perceive clearly, or get hold of: as he is glimpsed only through the mists of the narrator's neuroses, this may be deliberate. On the other hand, the portraits of James's wife Lucy and of Jane's own mother are sharp enough. Margaret Drabble seems consistently better at female characters than at male ones. But the presentation of James is the only artistic problem she fails to solve in this exquisitely constructed book.

The artistic strength of *The Waterfall* lies both in its technical skill and in its honesty. It shows us Jane winning through, painfully, to a rejection of puritanism while still acknowledging its force. The cost of following one's instinct for survival through love, against the moral code, into deceit and selfishness, is powerfully dramatised and honestly faced. In *The Garrick Year* it was suggested that things could be put right by finding nature and following it. The resolution of Emma's difficulties, though, is facile compared with the greater complexity and psychological depth of *The Waterfall*. This is Margaret Drabble's neatest exposition of her central concern, and paradoxically the most conclusive in its dramatised recognition that there is no true solution to the conflict between instinct and morality.

This conclusion, arrived at by a different route, is also that implied in *The Needle's Eye*. Like Jane, Rose has to face the inescapability of suffering, whichever moral choice one makes, though *The Needle's Eye* is a severe indictment of the unnecessary suffering caused by "life-denying" Evangelicism, from which Rose has to make a partial escape. Rose never becomes fully free, and goes on suffering, but she does find the courage to act against her conditioning. In *Jerusalem the Golden* it is not Clara who pays the price for her self-assertion, but those she comes into contact with. But the price has always to be paid.

Rosamund finds, breaking the moral code, that she cannot emancipate herself from it fully, either. Rosamund learns to love her baby, to care passionately for the child's survival, but she remains content to equate selfishness with "maturity." Rose's development takes her further: she recognises that in withdrawing from society, from "community," she was wrong, but her return to marriage, love and duty brings her no happiness either. Like Jane, Rose suffers mental disturbance. Both women find partial healing in returning to relationships with other people. *The Needle's Eye*, with its central theme of community, receives fuller treatment in Chapter 11.

While explicit general statements are scattered through the books, it would be dangerous to assume that they represent the views of the author: many of them are put into the mouths of first-person narrators, telling us about their attitudes. Frequently these narrators are contradicted, either by themselves, by other characters, by patterns of imagery (see Chapters 9 and 10) or by developments of plot (see Chapter 8). Margaret Drabble forms satisfying representations of social reality, expressed in an increasing command of moral paradox. In her work as a whole, we find a coherently developing world view (see Chapter 7) and interests which stretch beyond social morality to concerns of the spirit, of man's place in the universe.

2

Puritan ethics: a Victorian legacy

Being a Victorian at heart, I paid the Victorian penalty.—
Rosamund, *The Millstone*

All Margaret Drabble's characters are searching for values to
live by in a period of shifting moral codes, when the rules they
learned are being constantly rewritten. As they work their way,
searching for their identities, through contemporary moral
decisions, the author is weighing up the advantages and disadvantages of the puritan inheritance, surviving in the social morality
handed down to us from the Victorians.

Margaret Drabble understands and dramatises the lingering
effects of this inheritance, which her characters have to modify, if
not totally reject. This modification can be achieved only with a
struggle. Her leading characters are all reluctant puritans, who
must emancipate themselves. It is a reasonable assumption, given
her Quaker background, that this struggle, played out in all her
books, is her own. Characters have to grow into independence,
and in doing so become necessarily selfish. Rosamund achieves
selfish independence, but does not progress beyond it. Jane's
passion for James is selfishly based, but releases her power to
love. The selfishness is a necessary stage of evolution in the characters. Only when they have found the courage and determination
to act, independently of the framework of rules they have been
conditioned to accept, thus following as far as possible their own
natures, can they proceed to the next stage: discovering in themselves the power to love.

Rosamund, the least happy and fulfilled of Margaret Drabble's
heroines, describes herself as "a Victorian at heart" and none

of the characters is untouched by residual Victorian morality. The most convenient formulation of the Victorian social morality which followed the Evangelical revival is that of Professor J. F. C. Harrison:

> . . . the ethical standards of unbelievers were the same as those of professed Christians. Their morality was as puritanical as that of strict church or chapel goers. They were models of rectitude in their devotion to duty. To this code of belief and ethics, followed by Christians and unbelievers alike, we may give the name evangelicalism. In the previous generation the Evangelicals had been a group of devout, Calvinist-minded reformers within the Anglican church. But for the Victorians, the values with which the Evangelicals were associated had become an orthodoxy, and evangelicalism (Christian or secular) part of the ideology of the age . . . for the middle classes, evangelical fervour could find an outlet either in a philanthropy calculated to mitigate, without changing, the basis of the evils of industrial society, or in schemes for radical social reform . . . one of the social effects of Evangelicalism was to internalise the puritan values of hard work and self-reliance, and to inculcate a strong sense of duty. . . . Improvement was the key to success in life, the secret of how to get on . . . two dominant themes ran through all this advice: the gospel of work and the doctrine of self-help.
>
> Such effort was indispensably linked with application . . . in relation to this central aim of independence, the lesser virtues of frugality, self-denial and thrift stood as a means to an end . . . to argue that "Satan finds mischief for idle hands" or "Where there's a will there's a way" was to present a middle-class social outlook as the wisdom of the ages. . . . The religious doctrines of conversion, salvation and the millennium could be secularised to meet the needs of communitarian socialists; the promises and threats of Chartist orators were decked out in the imagery of the Book of Revelation or the language of the Old Testament. . . . The dissenting tradition (political, social and religious) . . . had been built by people who . . . were prepared to crusade against . . . injustices.

W. L. Burn (*The Age of Equipoise*) writes that self-denial was

> . . . deliberately practised, because it was held to be a moral value or because it was a necessary part of the process of self-advancement.

With hard work itself a virtue, postponement of present satisfactions for long term goals (in this world or the next), stoic endurance and renunciation were valued. These are recurrent themes in Margaret Drabble's fiction. Evangelicals spoke of "seriousness," a word constantly on the lips of her characters.

The tradition of Dissent "prepared to crusade against injustices" survives today in the remnants of Fabian socialism (dealt with in *The Millstone*) and what Jane in *The Waterfall* calls our "ridiculous liberal faiths." As many historians have pointed out, Socialism and the Trades Union movement are outgrowths of the social organisation of the dissenting chapel. Socialism and Trades Unions are examined in *The Needle's Eye*.

Noel Annan in his biography of Leslie Stephen, writes of the Evangelicals that through

> day to day meditation . . . Bible in hand . . . they learnt to train their conscience . . .

he adds that they were "constantly introspective."

Constant self-examination, the belief held by the Baptists and Quakers that God speaks through the conscience, can also lead to guilt and a conviction of punishment, which may manifest itself in an irrational fear of impending doom. Rosamund, Jane and Rose all suffer in this way. All Margaret Drabble's characters have eaten of the Tree of Knowledge in both the social and theological senses.

These nineteenth-century issues are recurrent themes in Margaret Drabble's books. She uses too, the imagery of the Book of Revelation and the language of the Old Testament. Biblical references and proverbs are scattered thickly through her works.

Theological vocabulary is used throughout her six novels: soul, conscience; suffering, sacrifice, martyrdom; sin, guilt, vice, wickedness, corruption; judgement, punishment, retribution, damnation; ignorance, illuminations; foreknowledge, predestination, election, free will; revelation, grace, redemption, enlightenment, salvation, providence; innocence, virtue, purity.

She moves outside the nonconformist tradition of theology for her invocations of penance and absolution, but keeps within its social values when writing of worldliness, hypocrisy, seriousness, earnestness, and reflects its social manifestation of improving

29

literature when writing of "moral fables." The words "puritanical" and "puritanism" are recurrent.

Margaret Drabble's characters lead bourgeois lives, often of quiet desperation. Her social panorama is mainly confined to the middle classes: there are no aristocrats in her books and only occasional forays into working class territory. None of her *dramatis personae* evinces the wilder manifestations of cultural, social or personal breakdown: none is promiscuous, nobody experiments with drugs or the occult (although the schizoid Jane in *The Waterfall* plays superstitious games with omens). Yet within these limitations, their plights reflect and crystallise for us our own. Margaret Drabble writes about what Paul Tillich (*Perspectives in Nineteenth and Twentieth-Century Theology*) calls the "conflicts between the religious tradition and the modern mind."

3

Conscience in action

She doesn't seem to hear any little whispers from the past ages of morality in the long night watches.—Sarah, *A Summer Birdcage*.

What else in life should one ever seek for but a sense of being right?—Rose, *The Needle's Eye*.

I thought now it was summer it was my duty to go for a walk.— Emma, *The Garrick Year*.

According to Max Weber,* the end of Puritan asceticism was to lead

> an alert, intelligent life: the most urgent task the destruction of spontaneous enjoyment . . .

Margaret Drabble's leading characters all try to lead alert, intelligent lives. Hard work, self-reliance, duty, thrift and self-denial are the values in the minds of all of them, though some of them kick against this ethic. The conflicting claims of duty and, to use the word in its popular sense, instinct, which seeks spontaneous enjoyment, are the stuff of her books.

The first three novels have first-person narrators; three very different heroines indulge in introspection and examine their consciences, which as we shall see are formed by the Victorian internalised social ethic. In the next three novels, there is less explicit examination of social puritanism, but it has not disappeared. *Jerusalem the Golden*, the fourth novel, has an omniscient narrator and examines the modern vision of heaven as a climb up the educa-

* *The Protestant Ethic and the Spirit of Capitalism.*

tional ladder.* *The Waterfall* alternates first and third person narration, *The Needle's Eye* has another omniscient narrator. The first four heroines are robust: they can cope with life's difficulties and more or less surmount their problems. The last two are driven to neurosis by religious guilt: they are thrifty, both of them, to the point of pathological meanness, and both practise futile renunciations.

The first heroine-narrator, Sarah, down from the comfortable "womb" of Oxford, has frittered her time as an *au pair* in France. She is paralysed by conflict, for although she has the puritan urge for self-advancement, for success and its fruits which she feels are due to her abilities, she is restrained from pursuing success too ruthlessly by her puritan conscience. In addition, she has to cope with her instinctive nature, "the pulls of sex and blood."

She feels herself subject to "subversive capitalist pressures from magazines like *Vogue*"; she doesn't know why she always punishes herself—she can't enjoy anything unless she does it the hard way. She hates wasting time without knowing why.

Professor Harrison may be able to supply an answer:

> Punctuality and early rising were essential in young people. So were the habits of orderliness—for just as genius seldom dispensed with the need for hard work, so success was seldom achieved by accident. Leisure was not to be wasted, but used.

Sarah's moral streak is "ravenous and demanding." Unlike a schoolfriend working as a probation officer, whose "moral streak has come out on top," Sarah cannot satisfy hers with a sacrifice. She compromises by filing things at the BBC. Her sister Louise, who lacks her puritan conscience, is a raving beauty and "always picks up wealth." She works in advertising after leaving Oxford and marries for money, deserting the man she truly loves.

"Louise, teach me how to win," Sarah says, "teach me to be undefeated, teach me to trample without wincing. Teach me the art of discarding. Teach me success." She envies success, but it

---

* "Ignorance is the curse of God: Knowledge the wings wherewith we fly to heaven."—Birmingham printer in the eighteenth century, quoted by J. H. Plumb, *In the light of history.*

frightens her: "Success is always scaring, particularly to the ambitious."

Later she muses, "I was playing at being a herbivore for a while, and gazing with admiration into the dangerous caves of the fiercer breed. I didn't mind. It soothed my conscience. Perhaps I am a herbivore at heart, and only predatory by conviction."

She may be right about this, for whereas Louise cynically denies the dictates of her heart for money, Sarah dismisses the richest man she meets as "boring." But despite being unable to sell herself for money and what it can buy, she takes a keen pleasure in chocolate, whisky (a taste she chooses at one point to dissemble), hotels, making eyes at passing men, rides in cars and expensive meals. She doesn't want to gain "nearly everything—one might lose the tiny, exhilarating possibility of one day miraculously gaining the whole lot."

Her sister, with almost unlimited money to spend on clothes, says, "I only want the things I can't have, model dresses and coats and things . . . one thinks there is a top, but there isn't." Another time, she says, "I must have clothes. I'm only young once . . . and if I don't have clothes now I'd feel I wasn't paying a debt to nature. And other things like food and theatres, I feel I must have them."

Sarah has a different morality: the word "adultery" (which Louise has committed with John) sends a "real Old Testament thrill" through her. She replies: "I feel I must have them, but I tell myself I'm wrong. . . . Didn't you feel you were being wicked?"

She knows Louise thinks her mad to prefer the "dirt and weariness and loneliness" Sarah is prepared to suffer "in order to gain a sense of hope." At university, Sarah had thought that "anybody can do anything," but later finds life not so easy.

Louise's fate vindicates Sarah's moral doubts. Her husband turns her out without a penny, naked under her dressing gown, when he finds her with her lover. Louise's sad experience contradicts Sarah's early conviction that one could have things both ways. "I thought I'd be free to have my cake and eat it," Louise tells her. "To keep love as a sideline. Don't you ever marry for love, Sarah. It does terrible things to people." Louise, despite having suffered, remains cynical.

Despite Louise's calculating nature, Sarah respects her sister's integrity: "She's not in any sense a frivolous person . . . we are both serious people." Sarah is self-reliant, proud of her independence. She thinks it all very well for Louise to make herself a living out of Stephen's books, but fails to see why she should experience "spurious and vicarious satisfaction on their behalf. I am far too conceited to take any true pleasure out of any such connection."

Chastened by being thrown out, Louise herself takes a moral view. She says her husband pretends he's making all his money out of his books, when in fact he "couldn't keep himself in socks off them. He lives off his father's tobacco factory . . . his double thinks on lung cancer . . . have to be heard to be believed."

Sarah's early conviction that "Louise always wins . . . and I lose" is shown to be wrong. Louise, when she breaks the rules of conscience, denying her own nature in marrying for money, receives a cruel comeuppance.

It is not hard for young women just down from university to identify with Sarah, in her consciousness of brains and attractiveness, but without much idea what to do with herself. Emma, in *The Garrick Year*, a beautiful girl whose ambitions are thwarted by her husband's career, and who finds herself trapped in the provinces with two babies to care for, is in a situation which makes her, too, easy to identify with.

In Emma, Margaret Drabble has created an eccentric and individual woman. Although there cannot be many personalities resembling hers, her conflicts are those of her generation. Emma is not a graduate, but a drop-out from an academic Cambridge family. She, too, went abroad to fill in the time between school and marriage.

Emma has married in haste and repented at leisure: the commonplace, she observes, enshrines a truth. "Yet it was a good gamble we made, each thinking that the other possessed the wildness to which we wished to chain ourselves for ever." Emma's initial attraction to "wildness" is temporarily damped down when she is forced into "endurance," finding herself indeed chained to David.

Emma and David (an actor) live in affluence unbacked by

34

capital, extravagantly. Yet she is always puritanically trying to do without, just to practise, just in case. This annoys David, whose extravagance is one of the things she loves. It excites her, and Emma talks a lot about being excited. She imagines that she lives for excitement.

She is a more complex character than Sarah. Emma's strictness, despite her wilfulness, her longing for the cheap and flashy and thrilling, takes (as she says herself) a perverse form. She insists on having everything in the best of taste—but that taste must be different from everybody else's, to overcome her conviction of spiritual vulgarity.

Her husband asks her, "Bad taste isn't a crime, is it?" But Emma confuses taste with worth and significance. Dressed in tatty antique clothes picked up on stalls, she "had refused to wear the clothes that might have accounted for me, or to pursue the interests that might have created me. And I had ended a freak." This sense of being a freak is shared by central characters in later novels.

Emma knows her tastes and her life are "shallow": she likes "anonymity, change and fame." She feels in need of "a little cheap riot." She knows that pop stars and film stars and knights "don't count, but I am the perfect audience . . . I depend. On the cheap, the louche, the tawdry, the shiny, the glistening caratless shammy selling line." She feels herself to be cheap and vulgar, despite her self-presentation in terms of eccentric distinction: all she wants is attention.

She has a tantalising opportunity to read the news on television, a part-time job which would enable her to fulfil her "conflicting responsibilities." To be on television is the accolade in the swinging society she hankers for and whose values she so clearly shares. But the chance is withdrawn when her husband insists on a year's work in Hereford.

Emma loathes Hereford: the provinces have never appealed to her "except as curiosities." Her preferred anonymity is that of a big city—she hates Hereford because it has a "fully occupied and classified air. Unlike London, it left no room for the placeless." She both enjoys and hates her alienation because it frees her from "classification" and yet leaves her isolated.

She exemplifies modern urban rootlessness: her urge to express

herself in sixty-year-old hats picked up for shillings is a manifestation of her longing to find some link with the past.

Despite her utter contemporaneity, Emma too has residues
from the Victorian past in her. Lacking interests of her own, she
admires achievement: Dr Leavis, Angus Wilson and "those others
who have really done real things." She has an arbitrary eclectic
moral compulsion, although she denies traditional moral values.

> We went to the chemist's to buy a packet of Kleenex, which
> I did not really need, but I always feel that I should avail myself
> of the facilities of public places.

She feels it her "duty" to go for a walk in summer; her lover,
Wyndham, asks her, "Is it a permanent trait in your character,
this desire to tell people their duty?" She also remarks, puritan-
fashion, "I was in debt and do not like to leave my debts beyond
the end of the week." Here there is a concealed irony: she has
been eating meals out at Wyndham's expense, and the debt she
owes him is adultery.

When Wyndham finally succeeds in seducing her (while she is in
bed with a cold) she thinks she might as well give in: she has no
interest in a purely technical chastity.

> For we are what we seem to be . . . so I let him get on with it,
> and I wish to God that I could say that I enjoyed it.

In granting validity to "seeming," we have Emma's surface
morality: she imagines she is preoccupied with shiny surfaces.
Yet the reference to God is not merely colloquial, and when she is
injured accidentally by Wyndham's car, whose speed and power
have been an explicit symbol of his appeal to her, she feels she
has been punished. Wyndham tells her, "You're a child . . . you
think you can take everything and give nothing."

She concludes that she has gone wrong:

> I could have loved him . . . I had opened myself either too little
> or too much, I had not faced the choice I should have faced, and
> I had ended up with neither fidelity nor satisfaction.

Emma as a child enjoyed swimming out of her depth, without
footholds. Yet if she imagines she can take all and give nothing,
she can recognise this dangerous morality in others: her husband

has always liked to think he can have the best of both worlds, that he can bite with impunity the hand that strokes him.

She can recognise in others, too, a serious attitude to life and sees that for another friend, Mike Papini, life was

> a discipline, a search for values, an investigation of the soul, an apprenticeship to a trade, and all his aberrations were simply an effort, however strange, of the right way (sic).
>
> Whereas with Wyndham I felt that life was an entertainment.

At school Emma used to snigger over Wordsworth's poems, which she rejected in her desire to be different: with a revulsion for what she most liked, she wanted to give it a good kick in the teeth for the sake of the Victorian virtue of independence.

At the end of the book, she weeps over Wordsworth:

> real wet tears . . . I weep partly as an apology for my past ignorance from which I might never have been rescued.

The trouble with *The Garrick Year* is that we remain confused as to which of Emma's various experiences has enlightened her. But well before she finds the maturity we are asked to believe she arrives at, she shows awareness of the orthodoxy she is trying to escape from. She has found her husband in the arms of Sophy Brent, an actress who "suffers the misery of wanting nothing but success, and not getting it." Emma, the theologian's daughter, says: "What about Sophy, then . . . the times I've put up with her pinching my cigarettes through Christian charity." She says to the doctor, "I know my soul's in a bad way, but what about my nose and my throat?"

> He had not expected too much of me, that doctor: he had not expected too much of my body, as my father had never expected anything of my soul. They were two professionals, those old men, and I lay back weakly, resting on their superior opinions of human limitation.

Margaret Drabble's characters all find out, more or less painfully, their human limitations, yet they all find in themselves an unsuspected strength, the power to survive.

Unlike Emma, Rosamund in *The Millstone* is not attracted by modern "decadence": she speaks of her "inherited nonconformist

guilt." The success she aims for is severely academic and strenuous: she can take no pleasure in the flesh, although she is good
looking, with "the hard fit shine of the well-nurtured."

She has a conviction that she has sinned, although her sin is

a brand new twentieth-century crime, not the good old traditional
one of lust and greed. My crime was . . . my . . . terror of the
very idea of sex . . . being a child of the age, I knew how wrong
and misguided it was.

She feels she carries on her bosom a scarlet letter, but her A
stands for Abstinence, not Adultery. As R. H. Tawney writes:

. . . the lean goddess Abstinence . . . the tutelary divinity of Victorian England . . . was inducted to the austere splendours of her
ascetic shrine by the . . . Puritan moralists.

"Permissiveness" has brought Rosamund no freedom: she
suffers for being a social misfit, and uses the words inherited
from an older morality. Its reversal does not free her from guilt,
which is felt by all Margaret Drabble's characters.

Rosamund dismisses the possibility that she might be pregnant
as "too ridiculous and unlikely a symptom of my sense of doom"
to be worth serious attention. She always has profuse images of
disaster.

Pregnancy is too much the kind of dream that her "nonconformist" guilt might be expected to project. Then switching from
the Victorian mode of thought to that of the twentieth century,
she wonders whether her symptoms might not be "purely psychological." She is caught at crisis point between these two cultural
habits, as most of us are.

Trained to examine her motives (which she does continually
throughout the book), Rosamund has to hammer out her own
moral values when she sees the one her parents taught her does
not fit the facts. Brought up a good Fabian rationalist, theologic-
ally she has rejected religion. But justice preoccupies her.

Although notions such as the afterlife and heaven seem to
her crude beyond belief, she fears that if her baby were to die
it would be a vengeance on her "sin." "What my sin had been
I found difficult to determine." Her puritan inheritance shows
in her conviction of guilt for unknown crimes, in her fierce inde-

pendence, in her reticence and scrupulosity, in her devotion to work.

When the baby is born, although she was at first unwanted, Rosamund feels love for the first time in her life.

> I had expected so little, really. I never expect much. The delight of holding her was too much for me, I felt . . . such pleasure should be regulated and rationed.

Having been taught to feed her baby only at regular intervals, she does not like to break the rules, although she knows this system is outdated. She doesn't want to wake the baby, either.

> So I put my head in the pillow, like a child anxious not to disturb its parents, and I cried.

In one of those neat, epigrammatic and profound summaries which make her so satisfactory a writer, Margaret Drabble continues in the persona of Rosamund:

> Authority, the war, Truby King. I was reared to believe that privation is a virtue and the result is that I believe it to this day.

By an ironic twist of characterisation, when Rosamund gets the baby home, she is conditioned by her hospital training, the "rules," and is afraid to feed the baby on demand, till scruffy, liberated Lydia, her novelist flatmate, advises her to.

Margaret Drabble, the creative writer, makes the imaginative leap of creating consequences which stem from the conflicts of Rosamund's upbringing. She is reared in upper middle class affluence and status, but the principles she is taught are inherited from the Victorian nonconformists (all upside down, in modern society, as Rosamund has always perceived, yet by no means dead).

It is the strength inherited from her puritan background which enables Rosamund to continue in a course which conventional puritan morality would condemn, and which even today, in our so-called permissive era, is not encouraged. Many people have illegitimate babies, but come up against immense social pressures if they want to keep them instead of having them adopted. Being the child of her parents, she accepts responsibility for her actions and refrains (in a poignant, but ambiguous, passage) from letting George know of his paternity. She doesn't want to encumber him—or share the joy of the baby with anybody else.

Intellectually arrogant, although hampered by diffidence, she muses: "Too much knowing is my vice." She coaches students, and charges too little, although it is pointed out to her that as a good socialist she is wrong to lower the price of her profession. She feels inadequate, although she knows she is well equipped.

> I suppose I taught because of my social conscience . . . I was continually aware that my life was too pleasant by half . . . I was born with the notion that one ought to do something, preferably unpleasant, for others.

She feels her students are her responsibility: three months pregnant, she is worried about them as "dependents." One of them is a Methodist minister, so Rosamund wears a curtain ring on her finger so as not to shock him "for his sake and not for my own." They are concerned not to embarrass each other: her corrections to his ill-organised, but well-read, essays are "always very tentative, as tentative as his references to God."

Sitting on a bus during her pregnancy, she gives in to the oblique nagging of two standing women.

> I had been reared to stand for the elderly on public transport . . . I heaved myself to my feet.

In these instances we see her devotion to duty and her inbred politeness.

She has a puritan sense of thrift, too. Asked whether she will announce her baby's birth in *The Times*, she says certainly, why not. But she thinks such announcements a waste of money: she is willing to flout convention by announcing an illegitimate birth, but unwilling to commit the financial extravagance. She grudges two pounds for a bottle of gin, hoping for an abortion, but when friends drop by the duty of hospitality leads her to offer it to them. Drinking the remains, she feels its nastiness is "some sort of penance" for her "immorality."

Anyway, her pregnancy seems to be the kind of event to which, however accidental its cause, "one could not say no." After her one sexual encounter with George, she chooses to believe that he does not wish to see her again, as this is "the most unpleasant conclusion"; she has to "prepare for the worst." She expects punishment, cannot relax or take life as it comes. Bulldozed by social pressures into an eventual experiment with sex, she keeps a virgin's reticence and self-containment. Pride restrains her from going anywhere she might bump into George.

Even this avoidance, however, takes on a "fearful moral significance." The geography of the district becomes "a map of her weakness and strengths," a landscape "full of petty sloughs and pitfalls, like the one Bunyan traversed." She means Bunyan's pilgrim, Christian, and the slip is significant, but the mention of Bunyan calls to mind archetypal Puritanism and a morbidly sensitive conscience. The reference also draws upon the ancient religious image of life as a journey, one in which the path is rarely smooth. Rosamund, like Emma, believes in walking, but enjoys car rides when they come her way.

Certain pleasures of the modern world appeal to her: she likes the "lovely gleaming spire" of Castrol House, all-night chemists, because they share the "irregular glamour" of all-night cafes, bars, airports and launderettes. These spots are all places where people meet each other, in contrast to her own painful isolation. While getting a prescription for her child, Octavia, Rosamund meets George for the first time since their sexual encounter, in an all-night chemist's.

Rosamund is always conscious that one must pay for whatever one has, yet when Octavia goes into hospital for an operation and is soothed by the doctor, Rosamund reflects, in Biblical phrase, "Flesh is weak, and we ask for too much, but it's a comfort when we get it, and without paying." She is thinking of the Health Service, on one level; but at a deeper one she is thinking about the moral balance of payments. Her parents are Fabian economists, with a nonconformist inheritance. There is more behind Rosamund's conditioning than Truby King.

The only Margaret Drabble heroine explicitly aware of her Victorian heritage, Rosamund reminds us constantly of Leslie Stephen, as described in Noel Annan's biography.

Impelled by his Evangelical heritage, he searched his soul for faults and tried to change himself but sought peace in work. He quoted Carlyle: "Properly speaking, all true Work is Religion." He believed in "discipline and self-reliance." Rosamund shows these traits and buries herself in her work. Leslie Stephen thought that people did not really like him, "so I will retreat from society and secure myself from any rejection which would mortally wound me." Rosamund never admits that she might be unpopular, but she too retreats from society, particularly George's, for fear of being rejected and hurt.

Annan says of Stephen, a militant agnostic like Rosamund,

> . . . we appear to have travelled far from the beliefs of Clapham. And yet there is still the belief in right conduct, in the same ethical standards.

Leslie Stephen rejected his religious heritage, that of the Clapham sect, but retained its ethical standards. Rosamund criticises the values she has been taught, but maintains, even in bringing up her baby, her parents' ethical standards, which have their roots in Victorian secularised Evangelicalism. Margaret Drabble ultimately shows these ethics to be inadequate for a fully human response to life, but they have their positive strengths: Rosamund has certain virtues.

In *Jerusalem the Golden*, set in a grim northern industrial town, Clara's background has only the negative aspects of Methodism. Like Rosamund, she rejects her background, but, like Rosamund's, it gives her the necessary toughness to survive.

Clara's scruples are social rather than moral, but come from this puritan home background. She is embarrassed about ordering drinks, although she likes drinking, and about asking for the Ladies. Going home to a miserably dry family reunion she thinks how much a drink would have helped. To her, a dinner jacket is "outlandish and embarrassing"; she is too prim to do cartwheels, although she can, "because my pants would show."

Dressed in safe, unobtrusive clothes, she realises that there are flights of fashion she hasn't the courage to try herself: but only social conditioning restrains her. She

> had and she felt slightly uneasy about admitting it, sought the smartly intense, at the expense of the more solid and dowdy virtues; she had been attracted by surfaces, by clothes and manners and

42

voices and trivial strange graces . . . she was drawn unquestionably to the surface of things.

We are reminded of Emma, but Clara's motives are different: she admits to her married lover, Gabriel, that all he is to her is "a means of self-advancement"; she realises others might see this as "decadence." Self-advancement is within the puritan ethic; a preoccupation with "surfaces" is not, which accounts for Clara's unease and her feeling she might be "decadent."

Margaret Drabble's characters condemn themselves when they admit to a previous attraction to "surfaces." Her own puritanism is in evidence here, in that the author, too, seems to agree that such frivolous attraction is culpable.

Like her parents, Clara is mean. She never entertains, though she is a frequent guest, and is not sure whether the cause is "avarice, idleness or sheer social ineptitude," but her conscience suggests they are all reasons "base enough to be true."

She uses the local bookshop as an "unofficial free library" and stands for hours surreptitiously reading. When she wins a state scholarship, "the cash payment spoke to Clara's industrial heart decisively." She is the child of the industrial north, with all its self-reliance, effort and thrift which verges on meanness.

Literature is Clara's escape but it doesn't take her far away from home. The Victorian children's books she reads, Sunday school prizes won by her mother, "preached the lessons of moderation, cleanliness, simplicity, self-denial and humility, low church to the core."

She enjoys the messages of Wayside Pulpits, not because she has any faith, but because they are phrased with some beauty.

> They were made up of words that seemed to apply to some large and other world of other realities, and they bore witness also to the fact that somebody had thought it worth his while to put them up. Just as some would pay for intelligence, so would others pay for the spirit.

The messages offer "some kind of alternative," so although Christianity means nothing to Clara she is glad it exists. Whether or not Margaret Drabble's characters recognise the spiritual world, it is always there in her books as a background to their lives.

Clara's diligence and frugality, so strongly marked in her

characterisation, and attributed by Weber to the Methodists, are her means of escape from an industrial, secularised Methodist background. Every detail of Clara's motivation and attitudes is accurately delineated.

Her lover recognises in her a "voracious simplicity, a need that did not pay too much attention to the sources of its satisfaction . . . for such a nature as hers, the sordid, if it existed, could not repel . . . hesitation only could repel." The "simplicity" of Clara's needs is a different thing from the "simplicity" preached in the Sunday school prizes of her childhood

Although the only God Jane in *The Waterfall* admits to recognising is Necessity, she is preoccupied with predestination and anxious about salvation. (She often rationalises these obsessions in Freudian, environmental or hereditary terms.) She has been brought up a middle-class Anglican, but harks back to the grim doctrines of Calvinist theology:

> If she was chosen, she was chosen: if not, then she would quietly refrain from the folly of asserting her belief in her election, in the miraculous interventions of fate on her behalf . . .

Jane's husband has left her and, characteristically turning her aggression upon herself, she is convinced she has "murdered" him by coldness and neglect. She seeks punishment for what she considers her crimes, and casts herself in the role of a "sacrifice." Jane practises renunciation to the point of withdrawing completely from life, staying in her house alone, spending as little as possible.

Her isolation is relieved by her affair. Jane feels she is embracing "corruption" in committing adultery and is to the end unsure whether or not James brought her "sexual salvation."

> James redeemed me by knowing me, he corrupted me by sharing my knowledge. The names of qualities are interchangeable: vice, virtue: redemption, corruption: courage, weakness; and hence the confusion of abstraction, the proliferation of aphorism and paradox. In the human world, perhaps there are merely likenesses. Recognition, lack of recognition.

This confusion mirrors her state of mind. She seeks virtue, but does not know how to go about it. Not generous or secure enough to act, she makes a virtue of "the hair shirt, the sack cloth."

Convinced of the "corruption of everything pertaining to the flesh," like the puritans described by Weber, and obsessed with original sin, the curse of Adam, she seeks innocence in abnegation, which she later realises is a sick withdrawal. As a child, her worst fear had been solitary confinement: as an adult, she chooses it, partly to punish herself and partly because she is afraid of life.

Going mad, she sees her madness in perverted moral terms, involving the puritan guilt at wasting time.

> I think . . . that such things as cooking are an evasion, they are a wrong use of time, time so pure, so precious, so reserved: for what? For nothingness, for solitude, for boredom, for silence.

There are "no angels, no ladder" when James comes into her life, but she demands him, despite all her efforts at self-denial. She reflects that her terms "salvation" and "damnation" are "hysterical, religious" ones. "But then life," she says in Evangelical vocabulary, "is a serious matter."

When James's car crashes on the motorway north of Stamford, Jane sees it as "a judgement" on them both, an "Act of God." She becomes convinced that there is "no nonchalance without squalor or cruelty, no passion without its accompanying neglect." She knows it is her "duty" to ring her cousin Lucy and James's parents, but is afraid of telling the truth. Eventually her sin finds her out and Lucy telephones her.

As James lies unconscious in hospital, Jane feels her faith will keep him alive. Yet she feels she lacks faith, and suffers from a conviction of sin. Even happiness seems to her to be "like some inevitable doom." She admires the human spirit for maintaining "its ridiculous liberal faiths," and lives in a state of terror and confusion.

"All unhappy individualities are related to a false impression received in childhood," writes Kierkegaard (*Journals*, 1849). SK's traumatic disillusion with his father's morality, his self-chosen isolation and his vocation as a writer make him relevant to Jane, as we shall see (Chapter 7).

Kierkegaard also wrote (*Journals*, 1844) that "The hardest

trial of all comes when a man does not know whether the cause of all his suffering is madness or guilt." This is Jane's characteristic form of trial.

She reflects that her husband Malcolm's "kindly instincts were deformed by our mutual guilt." Choosing him, she thought she was safe, denying herself tragedy, avoiding the "bloody black denouement that I had been sure, as a girl, would be mine." It had been "treachery" to think she could avoid this agony. But she ended up by winning from Malcolm "his hand in marriage, his peace of mind, his self-respect, his hope of salvation." She thinks Malcolm lucky that her neuroses are the reverse of extravagant: expenses are cut to bare survival level.

When her husband leaves her, she refuses even to take her son Laurie out to play, as she is pregnant and unwell.

> But her weakness tormented her: she knew that some effort was demanded of her, some heroic sacrifice.

Yet when she is called upon to sacrifice James, she fails to do so, and is (she feels) consequently punished. "Better to lose than endure the guilt of winning," she thinks.

At the end, she wonders why she was always so interested in being "innocent": she doesn't like guilt, she doesn't like being human, nor her own actions. But she refuses to take pills prescribed for her, loyal to her "religious dislike of cure." Her last words are: "I prefer to suffer, I think." Modern society allows no room for puritan guilt: but it exists, and the sufferer has to find some accommodation or go mad. Jane does go mad, though eventually she makes a partial recovery.

The puritan heritage is split in *The Needle's Eye* between two main characters. Simon's is merely ethical, Rose's is explicitly religious. Simon is an unbeliever, a lawyer, preoccupied by justice but unillumined by love. He acts only from obligation, without charity, although he knows that this is "no salvation." This effort destroys his emotions and he seeks for "grace." Aware of the meanness of spirit in him, he is afraid, like Jane, that his wickedness will flow from him and infect others.

He keeps going by concentrating on work, puritan fashion. His work as a barrister specialising in Trade Union law isn't even the work he wants to do. Simon exhibits the Old Testament morality, the "self-righteous and sober legality" which Weber describes as characteristic of the "worldly" Protestants.

The major decisions of Simon's life, his career and his marriage, have been made through lack of "spontaneous love." His mother has pushed him up the ladder from poverty, and he has married a rich girl as "the opposite" of his guilt-ridden childhood. His father-in-law's mail order business is not illegal: "it was simply, in Simon's admittedly puritanical view, unethical." Julie spends recklessly, and Simon judges himself for having admired careless spending. The longer he lives the surer he is that the golden mean has more to do with meanness than extravagance.

He is horrified at his wife's crude language: their classy friends speak as she does

> but to them the words came naturally, whereas to her they came with an air of defiance and genuine venom.

Simon disapproves that his friends are quick to ask him to dinner while his wife is away. He has little sympathy with women who grumble about living in a world without rules, because for him one rule remains: a man must make the first move.

Young middle-aged people "discussing sex with . . . a mixture of self-congratulation, envy, yearning and nosy vulgar curiosity" sicken him. Unhappily married, Simon has fantasies of women in black lacy underclothes, but is disgusted by the thought of contact. A working-class boy in upper middle-class society, Simon finds it difficult to know what is expected of a man, these days. He can relax only with the scruffy, well-bred Rose and Emily, both worn, déclassées, and authentic.

Rose, too, has marital troubles and finds it a satisfaction that Simon, "a serious person," would have liked to marry her had he been free. She herself married to show she was "serious." Rose is in the Margaret Drabble heroine's characteristic plight: intellectually she rejects, but inside herself accepts, the grim religious doctrines of the woman who looked after her. She knows that Noreen "corrupted" her, but is powerless to free herself. Noreen was, says Rose, "very puritanical"; elsewhere she is described as "grim, Evangelical, life-denying."

Noreen's doctrines are those that Victorian liberals, according

47

to Walter E. Houghton (*The Victorian Frame of Mind*), managed to escape from. He writes of "the old theology . . . in its popular puritan form," its "emotional fears as well as intellectual difficulties." We recognise in his picture the one Noreen presented to Rose:

> The conception of a jealous God of wrath, punishing most of the human race with eternal torture in hell, and of human nature innately corrupt and powerless to attain salvation except by an act of divine grace; the anxious self-examination in a frantic effort to determine whether one was among the elect or the damned; the realisation that the slightest moral failing or the least theological error was a dangerous sin—all this formed a context of living fear from which any escape, even at the cost of all religious faith, might seem at times a blessed event. And once freed of this "fatalist creed" one might experience an upsurge of fresh energy and self-reliance.

In its essentials, this is the "fatalist creed" shared by Jane and Rose. Neither attains complete freedom from it.

Like Emma, Rosamund and Clara, Rose concludes that she was destined to be some kind of "freak." Rose is an heiress and terrified that she will not get to heaven. "What can I do to be saved?" she cries.

As a child, she hears a sermon about the camel and the needle's eye, and although the clergyman is careful to apply modern Biblical scholarship and rationalise the story, Rose is convinced that his attitude is "casuistry." To her it is like the road to Damascus: "a horrible heavenly light" shone on her. Noreen, asked what she thought of the sermon, replied that if Rose wanted to believe that kind of soft soap she could. "Oh she was a dreadful woman, Noreen. But she was right," says Rose.

Convinced of the wickedness of riches, Rose like Jane tries renunciation but like Jane fails. She writes a cheque for twenty thousand pounds to build a school in Africa (which is burned down in the ensuing civil war), divorces her husband and chooses to live with her three children in a slum district of London.

When Simon first sets eyes on her, he remembers her as "the girl who gave all her money away to the poor, or something

48

ridiculous like that." Rose is "unassumingly correct": she has
the puritan virtues of a "calm diligence" and humility.

> It was on faith, not on evidence, that she operated after all . . .
> Rose believed in faith, as well as in works, that giving is not simply
> for the benefit of the receiver.

This, as Margaret Drabble puts it in a characteristic ironic twist,
is "an ancient orthodoxy, a modern heresy." All the Christian
denominations traditionally insisted that faith was necessary for
salvation: the controversy was as to whether works were irrelevant
(as Luther considered them), or "pleasing and acceptable to God
in Christ and do spring out necessarily of a true and lively Faith"
(*The Thirty-Nine Articles*: Article XII, Of Good Works). Good
works, says the Article, "cannot put away our sins, and endure
the severity of God's judgement." But in the modern secularised
world, only good works are valued: faith has become a heresy.
Terrified of God's judgement, Rose hopes that her good works
will be pleasing to God, because she has faith. But she has no
certainty. At the end of the book her "theological position" has
become a "neurotic heroic nonchalance." Her neurosis remains
with her.

Rose knows other people will see her as a crazed woman for
living as she does, denying her children for the "thin glamour
of an idea," like a Jehovah's witness or a Christian scientist refusing blood transfusions "for the sake of a delusion." Rose hopes,
with the Wesleyans, that even in this life it is possible to attain
freedom from sin by spiritual transformation, but, like Jane, she
has uneasy fears that the doctrine of predestination might be
true.

She finds some "inexplicable grace" in living the way she does:

> but as a nun attached significance to arbitrary vows, so she had
> attached it to this place that she inhabited . . . the rewards of
> faith had been hers . . . the sun . . . had shone forcefully upon
> her, it had illumined her.

She recognises, however, that she has cheated, financially by
keeping enough of her money to live on, intellectually by relying
on her friend Emily's children, "dirty, scruffy, jumble-sale dressed
little intellectuals", as companions for her children and by having

49

books in her tumbledown house. Her son Konstantin, a pre-
cocious six-year-old, who in the course of the book demonstrates
a wisdom beyond his years, calls her a "whited sepulchre." A
smaller, but more demanding, renunciation is asked of Rose:
eventually she sacrifices her withdrawal, her contented privacy,
and for the sake of her children takes back her husband. This
brings her no happiness, and she becomes more irritable with
the children, though she realises she has done her "duty." But she
has not, "after all, made the leap into clearer air."

Rose's puritanism, like Jane's, is more spiritual than social, but
she shares some puritan social attitudes with earlier characters.
She recognises that there has been "self-denial" in Simon's background; she has a moral objection to gambling (though she does
gamble at one point); disapproves of public libraries that classify
books under Light Romance. Rose does not bother to go to the
hairdresser; Rosamund and Jane disapprove of the waste of time
and money. Most of the heroines are concerned with "endurance":
Emma says stoicism is a virtue she can admire but not practise,
but admits to "endurance": Rosamund, Jane and Rose all make
a virtue of it.

Rose, like Jane, is convinced of the "irredeemability of her
own nature"; both compare themselves to nuns in their withdrawal from life. Both become pathologically mean and shabby.
Rose thinks, like Jane, that she can find innocence in abnegation,
self-sacrifice and withdrawal. Rose "did not forgive herself. She
was not much good at accepting, in herself, the natural short-
comings of humanity." Jane cannot forgive herself either: she has
an all-pervading sense of sin and corruption.

Jane and Rose share the Protestant dilemma: both anxiously
seek salvation, but for puritans there can be no hope of salvation
through the church and its sacraments, as there is in Catholicism.
Both try to practise the penitent humility that according to the
Lutherans could win back a state of grace. The relief of private
confession has been taken away by the Reformation, so Jane
writes an autobiographical novel, Rose unburdens her heart to
Simon. Jane and Rose both take up a puritan stance in rejecting
the Church of England's offer of comfort through the sacraments,
"which on those that worthily receive the same they have a
wholesome effect or operation" (Article XXV, Of the Sacraments).

Both these women wrestle, in puritan fashion, directly with God, without any priestly intermediary.

Preoccupations with election and damnation hardly seem pressing contemporary concerns. One suspects that having exhausted the theme of social puritanism, still very much alive, Margaret Drabble turns to its theology for material, although that theology is moribund, if not dead. Yet in giving two of her heroines Calvinistic visions of life, Margaret Drabble is able to continue her explorations of the conflict between puritanism and instinct. In Jane's schizoid state Margaret Drabble finds an adequate rationale for Jane's anxieties. Rose is less satisfactory as a characterisation, as she has to bear so great a weight of symbolic interpretation that our image of a personality is in danger of getting lost.

But puritanism appears in all of Margaret Drabble's leading characters, either in residues of the Victorian social ethic, or in the lonely individual soul, seeking its own salvation in the isolation created by the Protestant revolt.

4

Nurture

Children begin by loving their parents. After a while they judge them. Rarely, if ever, do they forgive them.—Oscar Wilde.

Empirical psychologists have collected much evidence to make it likely . . . that the conscience of a given individual is closely bound up with the affection that he or she received as a child.—Professor Henry Chadwick.

Dad, she said, can people help what they grow up like, or does it just happen? Of course they can help it, he said, lying bravely.—*The Needle's Eye.*

I am my parents' daughter, struggle against it though I may.—Rosamund, *The Millstone.*

Blood is blood . . . I repudiate them, with pain I do so, dangerously I do so: I repudiate in them the human condition, my birth, my sustenance. . . . It was all predestined . . . what faith I must have had to believe there was any hope of eluding the grip of environment.—Jane, *The Waterfall.*

The apple does not fall far from the tree.—Clara, *Jerusalem the Golden.*

Searching for their identities, Margaret Drabble's characters all struggle against their environmental conditioning at the hands of their parents, yet all eventually are forced to accept their inheritance. They arrive at acceptance that environment has made them what they are. This acceptance usually comes as a profound illumination about their own natures.

Sarah, returning home to her parents, prosperous but provincial Birmingham business people, thinks how pleasant and unobjectionable fitted carpets, fitted curtains, wall lights like candles and chiming doorbells really are. But she cannot stay at home with her possessive mother: she has to escape to London.

Yet when her sister telephones in distress, asking to come round, although Sarah has a man in her flat, she sends him away and accepts the bond of familial obligation. She takes in the sister she envies and who she feels dislikes her, because "blood is thicker than water."

Emma in *The Garrick Year* thinks her meanness and David's extravagance are probably due to her background of professional comfort and David's of poverty. Emma is attracted by a young man, and is delighted to say in recognition of something familiar, "My father is a don, too," and they compare backgrounds

> dominated . . . by the well-bred, the quietly discursive, the mildly permissive.

Emma's in-laws, Welsh nonconformists, are in puritan fashion shocked that Emma's theologian father is not teetotal, like them. "For a man who pretends to have faith," they comment, "he has remarkably little respect for the decencies of life." Without being aware of it, they are exhibiting a puritan concern with the virtue of sobriety, of right conduct in everyday life. David has understandably reacted against his "religion-ridden" childhood by ostentatious pursuit of drink and women.

Emma's mother was tubercular, "vivid and bony" and a drinker. But Emma has

> simply lifted from my background what I thought would be of use: an excuse for mild indulgence, a good sob-story to endear myself to people late on at parties . . . and a respect for my father.

She remarks that a life of discipline like that her own father led would hardly suit David. David is afraid Emma too is tubercular, but she remains healthy, although morally divided by her mixed inheritance.

Rosamund has the "hard fit shine of the well nurtured." Just as she is the most explicit and extreme example in Margaret Drabble's work of the puritan conscience in its contemporary manifestation, so she is the most explicitly analysed in terms of background.

"They had drummed the idea of self-reliance into me so thoroughly that I believed dependence to be a fatal sin," says Rosamund, the "good Fabian rationalist."

She is "well brought up," which has its advantages and disadvantages: she feels obliged to let people make demands on her without making any on them. Rosamund and her friends are all "scrupulous," a Victorian nonconformist word applied to anxiously examined consciences, in personal relationships.

Rosamund explains to George that her parents' consciences have an extraordinary blend of "socialist principle and middle-class scruple," carrying the more painful characteristics of their "nonconformist inheritance" into their political and moral attitudes. Rosamund's father is a professor of economics. The Stacey parents see life "through the eyes of Mrs Webb," in Annan's phrase: they go in for plain living and high thinking and they name their daughter Beatrice. They "crusade against injustices" in the dissenting tradition.

But despite their rejection of religious faith, their transference of belief in the millennium from religion to politics, they retain the Victorian puritan belief in self-denial.

> They have to punish themselves, you see. . . . They can't just let things get comfortable.

Rosamund realises that her family's values are an aberration. A rich Tory barrister friend is "all that my parents had brought me up to despise and condemn": Roger talks loudly in public places, is rude to waiters and people who try to tell him about parking his car. Her parents call such behaviour "vulgar," but Rosamund thinks it is "no such thing, except by a total falsification of the word's meaning." Rosamund recognises that her parents' standards, basically moral rather than social, are not observed by other members of their socio-economic group. By making manners a moral matter, she implies, they falsify meaning, making nonsense of her experience, just as they turned everything "upside down" by the way they educated her. Yet she cannot emulate Roger's rudeness and remains shrinkingly polite herself.

Her other pseudo-lover Joe (she pretends to each that she is sleeping with the other) is "pitted and scarred," while Roger is "a smooth man." Joe, a novelist with a working-glass background, has an attitude of

> defiant pleasure in his own successes: for years so unacceptable, his acceptability came to him not like Roger's as a birthright . . . but as a challenge. . . .

Each man believes the other to have a worldliness he himself lacks, and consequently envies and despises the other. This sets Rosamund's conflicts in a wider context: she isn't the only one to be caught between puritan contempt for "worldliness" and modern hedonism. Two men with very different backgrounds share her confusion because it is that of her generation: she is not a special case, merely an extreme example.

Lydia, another novelist friend, does not have Rosamund's "hard fit shine": her skin is grey, thanks to a childhood diet of "baked beans, bread and dripping and jelly." Although Rosamund's parents "grumbled incessantly" they did not do without. It takes Rosamund a long time to evolve an economic view of her own, because of the anomalies in her upbringing. (Rosamund the rationalist is fond of the word "anomaly.") Her nurture "had made me believe in the poor without being of them." Sent to "a very good grammar school," she is the only child whose parents vote Labour, although they are among the "poshest and most well-known of all."

She knows this is "upside down" and is confused by it.

Rosamund's father has gone to a new university in Africa as professor of economics, "to put them on the right track. He was on the right track himself, or he would not have been invited." Rosamund, despite her irony, has been born on the right side of the tracks, too, and although confused between her family's morality and the behaviour of others in her social class, is far from unappreciative of her "inherited prestige." She uses it shamelessly when she wants to visit her baby in hospital, and when the baby is born is conscious of going in the ambulance from a good address. She is interested in placing people socially, by their accents. Like Emma, she extracts what she can from her background.

She realises that if she had not been born and reared as she was, she would probably not have dared to have and keep the baby. She is cashing in on the foibles of a society which she has always distrusted. "By pretending to be above its structures I was merely turning its anomalies to my own use." She does not recommend her course of action to anybody less advantaged in the world than herself. When Joe appears on an "egghead TV programme" some of the other mothers in the hospital recognise him when he visits her; she is pleased that her "stock would rise" through the association.

Her parents combine social prestige with "practical earnestness." Rosamund's mother was a "great feminist" who used to quote Queen Elizabeth I's speech about being turned out of her kingdom in her petticoat to Rosamund and Beatrice when they were frightened about exams or going to dances. "I have to live up to her, you know," says Rosamund.

Although she consciously rejects much of the parental teaching, Rosamund remains under her mother's influence. The instance of Mrs Stacey quoting Queen Elizabeth's defiantly courageous words over such comparatively small hurdles as examinations or the even smaller ones of dances makes us smile. It also illustrates dramatically how all life's small ordeals were set, in the Stacey household, in a context of strenuous moral effort.

Annan sets the background for us:

> Evangelical parents guided their sons and daughters from infancy to distinguish between right and wrong, the good and the wicked, the precious and the worthless.

This is the tradition Rosamund inherits, unwillingly. To spare her embarrassment after she has the baby, her parents go on to India, leaving her their flat. She sees herself as emancipated woman, with her own key, but it is the key of her parents' flat. Significantly, she still lives in their home, and cannot emancipate herself from their influence.

> Their behaviour seemed natural to me, for I am their child, but I have speculated endlessly about whether or not they were right . . . such fear of causing pain, such willingness to receive and take pains.

But there are things in her that cannot take this morality. As a child, she used to put up with any discomfort, rather than cause offence. Now, with a child of her own, she finds she has to fight, or Octavia will suffer too. Yet the baby was named after a "heroine of socialism and feminism," the values her parents have taught her. At every turn Rosamund shows her inability to emancipate herself fully from the parental influence.

> I contemplated my growing selfishness and thought that it was probably maturity.

She thinks the way she was brought up was "probably right, but it didn't do me much good, did it?" She wonders whether her parents are to blame for her inability to see anything in human terms of like and dislike, love and hate, only justice, guilt and innocence.

Rosamund thinks that her parents are still children: they "think that they can remain innocent." She cannot take the patronising view of the Roman Catholic convert in Angus Wilson's short story about a similar couple and see them with tolerant affection as "darling dodos." Rosamund, with a nonconformist inheritance, has been taught to judge by her parents, and she judges them harshly:

> from a warm and fleshly point of view, they are perhaps as danger-ous and cruel as that father in Washington Square.

Dr Soper, we remember, denied his daughter any chance of sexual fulfilment, for reasons which were not wholly wrong.

Rosamund's parents, although always off stage, are clearly drawn for us, and their presence is felt throughout the book. We are haunted by our glimpse of Mrs Stacey, her hair skewered into a bun, leafing through a stack of probation reports.

Criticised harshly by Rosamund as they are, the Stacey parents in their social concern and public spirit, in their scrupulous con-sciences, have many of the positives associated with the dissenting tradition. They earn our respect.

Grim and grudging, mean financially and in spirit, Clara's mother in *Jerusalem the Golden* shows merely its negative aspects. Clara, whose name turns out to be a fortunate accident, an un-expected advantage, was named

> not in the vanguard but in the extreme rearguard of fashion, after a Wesleyan great aunt . . . as a preconceived penance for her

57

daughter . . . Mrs Maugham . . . chose it through a characteristic mixture of duty and malice.

Mrs Maugham is a brilliant creation: she stands in the gallery of appalling literary mothers with Mrs Bennett, Mrs Nickleby and Mrs Portnoy.

> She had been brought up as a chapel goer, and two generations back her family had been staunch Wesleyans, but she herself had long dropped any pretence to faith . . . and . . . considered all religious observation as a ridiculous frivolity. However, she retained the moral impetus of her early years . . . the narrow fervours and disapprovals were there, but their objects had subtly altered over the years.

In Mrs Maugham the puritan virtue of thrift becomes a perversion: she tries to teach her children, writes Margaret Drabble with devastating wit, that the "truly refined can manage without toys, clothes and entertainment"; the precise balance of economy and decency in her husband's coffin becomes a subject of "endless dissertation."

Telegrams in that family mean nothing but death, as nothing else is worth the expense. Mr Maugham had provided for his family "almost recklessly: in so far as a man may squander upon insurance, he had done so," says the author in one of her characteristic witty paradoxes. Clara's mother lets her go to Paris because it is "a bargain," though later she starts grumbling and raising complications.

> There was something in Mrs Maugham's conscious rectitude that threw a faint shadow of guilt over everyone who approached her. . . .

Clara, amazed at getting permission for the Paris trip, thinks "guiltily, I do not even feel guilty." Later, at university

> often, when drunk or naked,* thoughts of her mother would fill her mind.

But such thoughts impel her to continue on her course of escape.

Clara realises that her mother is "colossally inconsistent": Mrs

* A neat formula, this, for summing up Clara's extra-curricular activities.

Maugham does not even maintain the Methodist virtues of diligence and frugality which sustain her daughter. Although grudging about expenses, she is a shopper in department stores and can never resist their sillier gadgets. She says she hates clutter, yet her house is full of it. On her table is a slop basin with purple tulips, always laid. This embarrasses Clara, who knows nothing of the history of slop basins, nor of the society that produced them: she hates to see an "eccentricity erected into a symbol of the traditionally correct."

Mrs Maugham takes moral attitudes about having a telephone (good) and a television set (bad). However, when she gets her television, those who haven't got one are "highbrows, intellectual snobs or paupers." She refuses to have her husband cremated because she misguidedly imagines that cremation is a new-fangled idea. Clara longs for "marble angels wildly grieving" instead of the so-called good taste of economical restraint in tombstones. In Mrs Maugham the puritan qualities have decayed so that the environment she creates represents for Clara only a prison in which spontaneous enjoyment is impossible. Any possibility of instinctive life, of generosity, of warmth, is strangled. "Clara had affection in her and nowhere to spend it."

Her late father, employed at the Town Hall, had an 1895 edition of the *Encyclopaedia Britannica*, which he occasionally read.

> He would also exhort his children to read it, and laid great stress on the utility of information.

Professor Harrison writes of "the gospel of work and the doctrine of self-help": "Improvement was the key to success in life, the secret of how to get on." Clara learns this lesson when her parents allow her to go to Battersby Grammar School, the town's least distinguished. Mrs Maugham, although the kind of mother who turns down grammar school places because of the cost of the uniform, is in the wrong social position to do this to Clara.

Eventually, returning to find her mother dying of cancer, Clara recognises that the native town she hates so much is full of kindly people, and invites her lover Gabriel to see "a lovely teaset with tulips."

By this time she has learned to enjoy the arts, having achieved her secular heaven, friendship with a rich and cultivated family. She envies them their close warmth, their privileges. She realises, on her second trip to Paris, as Gabriel's mistress, that people who sit on expensive *terrasses* find it worth it to be there in the sun, and are not overcome with shock when they get their bills. Visiting Bond Street she wonders whether expense is not "the key to such charm."

Yet although membership of the Denham family, which Clara achieves through her liaison with Gabriel, who is unhappily married, seems to her like heaven, it has its disadvantages. Their world, unlike hers, is too comfortable and the Denham children, unlike her, cannot easily escape. Clara says to Gabriel that the family seems to be "rife with incest." Gabriel criticises his "kindly, charming, celebrated parents," who wanted their children to be "strange and wonderful": "all this affectionate uncritical encouragement, it can't be right, can it?"

Clara's friend Clelia is still living at home, although her siblings suggest it is time she left. Clara is amazed at the affection between Clelia and her sister Annunciata. Where she comes from, sisters are expected to be rivals until they have children. Her own home, even when there were two parents and three children in it, had seemed

pockets of isolated, self-contained, repellent activity;

the Denhams

seemed to be perpetually, intricately, shiftingly involved . . . with a whole circle of cross-threaded connections.

Yet watching Clelia and Annunciata, Clara is reminded of Christina Rossetti's "Goblin Market," a poem which emphasises the security of love and loyalty between sisters as against the dangers of involvement with "little men," who tempt with dangerous fruit which once tasted leaves a craving.

Gabriel's mother says her oldest daughter, Amelia, went "dotty because she can't have any children," but Gabriel, more perceptive, says:

"she went mad through the shock of waking up in the outside world, out of the golden nest, and she only married to get away

60

from us . . . to escape from our amorous family clutches . . . when she breathed the cold air of Essex she went mad."

Nevertheless, Clara envies people like Gabriel and Clelia: "Why do you all have such marvellous relatives and wives and husbands. . . . Why didn't I have a few? . . . what do you think of the ties of blood? . . . I believe in them."

Gabriel says it is "positively unnatural" for Clelia to be still living at home, but "she . . . couldn't afford such a nice standard of living anywhere else." Gabriel tells Clara that Clelia is gifted, but the rest of them "will never do anything." Without the abrasive impetus of hardship, these privileged children lack Clara's sense of direction.

When she gets back home, she looks at the "sad, much-hated objects of her infancy" and is frightened to think how much violent emotion she has wasted on them. She had not been condemned to them for life.

Looking through her mother's old photographs and diaries, and seeing that her mother too had once been intelligent and ambitious, she is

> glad to have found her place of birth . . . she felt, for the first time, the satisfaction of her true descent. There was no such thing as severance: connections endure till death and blood is blood.

Clara has achieved reconciliation of her two worlds. Clara can survive her mother's inconsistencies, but Jane in *The Waterfall*, like Rosamund, remains confused. Jane's father is headmaster of a small independent school, and her parents are petty hypocrites and snobs. They pay lip service, with puritanical hypocrisy, to the solid virtues, while hankering after "the vain honours and titles and glories" which, every speech day, they "solemnly denounce."

Poor Jane finds it hard to accept that her teacher father is not intelligent: it is "authority doubly betrayed." Her mother goes in for good works, makes charitable gestures, but the example of "good works" Jane cites is a negative and restrictive one, not a positive contribution.

> . . . she campaigns against . . . new public houses—she, who does not care for alcohol, she who has never set foot in a public bar

61

in her life. She campaigns against these things as the impotent campaign against sex and abortion.

In Jane's mother we see the combination of "good works," the social work whose nineteenth-century efflorescence was a direct result of the Evangelical movement,* and the Victorian obsession with "worldly success."

With her parents, says Jane, "awareness of rank was a disease." Her mother is considered charming, yet Jane would hear her

> in private savage, relentlessly, the antecedents of those very people she took such pains to charm. . . . "What you wear doesn't matter, it's what you *are* that counts," my mother would piously declare . . . casting appraising glances at . . . her acquaintances' coats. . . .

Her main value in life is respectability. Jane sees her parents' gestures of public spirit as hollow mockeries, but is afraid to repudiate her parents, "because in doing so I repudiate the human condition." Everywhere Jane finds a gap between her parents' professions and their real attitudes. She feels the landscape is "civilised out of its natural shape" because appearances bear no relationship to reality.

Despite their charitable gestures, Jane's parents lack all social sympathy. Their attitude to life is competitive. Jane rejects her parents' inheritance of worldly admiration for success, of social competition, of Pharisaism and cant. She overreacts against their coldness and falsity by withdrawing from the world.

But brought up on "Pharisaism and cant," she retains an emotional link between "cash and religion," a pairing which, according to Annan, characterised Victorian puritan attitudes. She thinks in mercantile metaphors of winning and losing, gambling, profit and loss, debit and credit, borrowing and lending, bankruptcy.

She extends these terms to cover her financial, social, sexual, moral and religious life. These metaphors are linked in her mind with her parents' legacy of "social competition," of petty niceties and distinctions, "cruel rejections," the "guilt of winning."

Like her parents, who envy the worldly glories they denounce,

* See K. Heasman, *Evangelicals in Action: An Appraisal of their Work in the Victorian Era.*

who say clothes don't matter and eye other people's, Jane in adult life hypocritically denies her desires. As a child, she chose "concealment and deceit." At another point she says she was "not a secretive child, merely unhopeful." Yet inconsistently she describes her childhood hopes of "an orgasmic moment" when she would become adult.

Grown up, before her disastrous marriage, in which she re-enacts her parents' own married misery, she declines a drink to "outwit my mother at her own abstemious game." Only by such deceitful gestures can she conceal her desires.

If I declined the permitted measure, how could they know how much and what I really wanted?

She attaches an undue weight of significance to James's action in helping himself to a second Scotch: in his "angel-like simplicity" she sees "the lovely flower of moral courage, so long sought." Jane oscillates between desire and abnegation and the alternation splits her in two.

Like Rosamund she equates selfishness with maturity, in that it shows an escape from parental conditioning. She wonders, similarly, whether her pleasure in her convenient likeness to her cousin Lucy, whose husband she has borrowed, indicates "maturity or total depravity."

Brought up on hypocritical and equivocal moral standards, Jane cannot find an acceptable morality, so clings in her search for certainty to obsessions with fate, election and predestination. But she receives only a dusty answer: she finds that moral choices must be made.

Jane's parents do not accept the values of the city. They live in the country and the idea of living in town is "morally abhorrent" to them. A divorce between Jane and Malcolm would "have finished" them: "divorce, unlike madness, was unknown in our family," which has "faintly clerical" connexions.

Jane sees, but is powerless to change herself, that her faith in life and in herself has been undermined by her parents' inconsistency in preaching one set of values and practising another. She perhaps does not see, though it is made clear to the reader, that her preoccupation with blood, doom and decay comes from an insecure childhood. Yet Jane knows she cannot repudiate the ties of blood, in the sense of kinship. She is convinced that her son is "doomed" because he is hers. She fears "human nature."

Her mother, who "flinched from every physical approach" was fond of saying, "Marriage and family warmth are *so* important." Touching between relatives is taboo in the Bennett family, among the Scotts in *The Garrick Year*, among the Maughams and among Jane's relatives. She hungers for and envies intimacy. Yet she and James, cousins by marriage, have never touched or kissed till he climbs into bed with her, and she enacts with her husband the cold destructive lovelessness she saw in her own parents.

Simon, in *The Needle's Eye*, is another "exile," this time from working class roots. He is full of resentment and comes to hate people. A "masquerader", he has suppressed his northern accent and feels that

> his whole life, the clothes he wore, the car he drove, the way he spoke, the house he lived in—was an act of misrepresentation.

Actually, Simon has two cars. Driving the big one he bought because his wife nagged him to get it and because he enjoys big cars, he feels he has fallen into corruption,

> enacting those old and preordained movements of the spirit, those ancient patterns of decay.

Always a climber, Simon (like his friend Nick) has joined the professional classes because their parents

> had bent on their sons the peculiar weight of their own thwarted ambitions.

His mother's house

> stank of cleanliness, of bleach and disinfectant . . . yet he was, no doubt about it, his mother's son.

Simon, too, must acknowledge his inheritance, though his lack of love comes in part from the harshness of his nurture. His mother's offering was "bleak, but if she had not aspired, she would have sunk or died." This driving, neurotic woman, true to the puritan ideal of self-advancement, has pushed him through direct grant school to Oxford. Simon feels impelled to submit to this pushing because of his obligation, because for years he has hated her.

The climb has been painful: Simon had to go to school in his father's cut-down suits. He reflects that his school, priding itself on providing for the gifted poor, had been good at making the gifted poor feel wretched. He realises that its true function had been to provide for the gifted middle class. He had "the worst of it all along, caught between reality and aspiration." Like Rosamund and Jane, Simon finds it hard to adjust to the gap between the picture presented by his upbringing and what he finds the world to be.

Trained by Mrs Camish's winces and shudderings, he remains his mother's son, and like her observes the social world with disapproving silence. Disliking this inheritance, he marries rich, vulgar Julie to escape such "deadly niceties and cruel rejections," seeking the same escape as Jane, who marries downwards in the social scale. He enjoys, at first, the tasteless opulence of Julie's home, the heart-shaped cover for the lavatory seat which he knows his mother would condemn.

Julie's house is a contrast to his grandparents' home, "oppressive, smelling of cats and bad cooking, and too full of deadly whiskery unfeeling menacing embraces." People like him, he reflects, who have grown up with too much physical intimacy, in cramped houses, can only wish to find large, empty spaces. But having found them, they long again for contact. The capacity, however, has been dissipated in the climb.

In his wife he finds "coarseness and coldness." In choosing her, he was conditioned by "psychological determinism." Condemned to "approach his own doom," he thus lived out his "hereditary destiny."

> Coarseness she had from his grandfather, coldness from his mother, and their good qualities she lacked.

Simon's marriage, made in rejection of his background, he later realises to have been dictated by it. His mother had fed him pelican-like with her own blood, cold though she had been. He muses that one can always tell when people are being psychoanalysed because they start abusing their mothers. Even his choice of career is determined by his background. He chooses union law as an acknowledgement of a debt to his father, victim of an industrial accident.

Rose's journey, in the same novel, has been in the opposite direction from Simon's. She has sought to move downwards, like Jane trying to renounce her heritage. Her indoctrination does not come from her parents, who largely ignore her, but from her mother-substitute, the Evangelical Noreen.

Rose makes discoveries: brought up in affluence and having chosen squalor to punish herself, she at first cannot understand why anybody should buy thin bedroom curtains which fail to keep out the light. Later she grasps that thin materials are cheaper than thick ones. She doesn't like thick fluffy towels that leave bits all over: she prefers threadbare, "hard rubby" ones like those in her slummy house. Rose reflects that with her background she can afford to wear a dress twelve years old—her neighbours can't.

Yet although she tries to reject her family, she can hardly prevent herself from taking some kind of credit when one of the visitors to her ancestral stately home praises the tea provided.

When the structure of the story demands it, even minor characters are firmly rooted in their socio-economic backgrounds. In *The Garrick Year*, Mrs Scott, mother of Emma's school friend, has the kind of mild face which shows a deliberate "evenness of life." Emma has seen such faces on headmistresses and others in positions of command, but never on the underprivileged.

Mrs Scott serves large prime joints and lives in "careful comfort" but without extravagance. "I always got the impression," says Emma, "that their household was governed by a mild and firm economy." Emma takes pleasure in shocking Mrs Scott by confessing that she has a French nanny. She knows that for people like the Scotts, rather irrationally, it is all right to have gardeners and domestic help, "but to have a nanny was as wicked as having a chauffeur."

Mrs Scott's daughter Mary is very much a product of her background. She represents middle class restraint, with its virtues and limitations. She is not particularly imaginative and believes that

really interesting people did not behave oddly, that oddness was a sign of insecurity, that true intelligence could satisfy itself perfectly well by orthodox means.

66

Mary makes Emma feel that her own desires, to be photographed and to appear on television, are "paltry, vain and valueless." Emma is in search of values, and the centre point of *The Garrick Year* is a meeting between Mary and Sophy Brent, a bad actress who nevertheless has bounce, wildness, an instinct for spontaneous enjoyment, an openness to life which Mary lacks.

> I could not deny . . . that I found her manner considerably nearer home than I found Mary's . . . I tried hard not to side with Sophy . . . I tried to balance myself neatly in the middle . . . I grew increasingly confused, as my ear gradually attuned itself to the differences of phrasing, vocabulary, sentiment and subject matter that separated my two guests.

In the end Emma, daughter of a theologian father and a drunken tubercular mother, chooses Sophy's world and knows that after Mary has seen Emma with her lover in a restaurant, she and Mary will never see each other again. Emma recognises in herself the "streak of flippant gloss" which attracts her to Sophy. It is, of course, her urge to spontaneous enjoyment.

Habits and beliefs, in Margaret Drabble's world, are socially conditioned. Although the characters struggle against this conditioning, intellectually rejecting their parents' values, the choices they make are initially dictated by their inherited morality, if only in reaction against it. And the morality they inherit, however transmuted or even perverted, is basically a puritan one.

5

Educated women

When the Welfare Officer . . . called on Rose, she . . . felt guilty because she was reading the *Guardian* instead of scrubbing the floor.—*The Needle's Eye*.

We were both predestined from birth, by ambitious parents, for university.—Jane, *The Waterfall*.

I cannot think why I was so certain at first sight of her relative stupidity: it . . . cannot have been the old adage about beauty and brains, which I have seen disproved both ways often enough. —Emma, *The Garrick Year*.

You can't be a sexy don.—Sarah, *A Summer Birdcage*.

She handled her apparatus with the efficient familiarity with which other women handle their baking boards and rolling pins; years of housework had left their mark on her.—*Jerusalem the Golden*.

Do not adjust your set: reality is at fault.—Graffito.

Sarah, Emma, Rosamund, Jane and Rose all come from comfortable backgrounds. Neither Emma nor Rose goes to university, though their parents could well afford to send them. Sarah and Jane are Oxford graduates, Rosamund a Cambridge graduate on her way to a doctorate.

Clara and Simon have to fight their way to university, but from backgrounds not too far down the social scale: neither is really underprivileged. Clara is lower middle-class and inherits, like Simon, a northern grit which impels her to succeed. Simon's father is a factory worker, but his mother is a grammar school product, and she drives him to Oxford, choosing the Bar because it is the most expensive profession. Clara, accepting the values of the city, reaches London University. All the characters who have been to university are moulded by it as a formative experience.

Graduate disillusion is indeed a part of Margaret Drabble's material. As she perceives and dramatically expresses, higher education, the Mecca of so many intelligent girls, is only a beginning. There is a temptation to use it as a temporary refuge, but afterwards the real problems of life have to be faced. The present generation of educated women find in her portrayals truth to their own experience.

Sarah's reminiscences of university friendships include coffee, *Beowulf*, relics of past essays, patterns for wedding dresses, scraps of material and ideas for bouquets from *Vogue*.

> I discussed these things . . . with much greater concentration than I could summon up for . . . revision.

This passage stirs nostalgic reminiscence in university women, who admit to identifying with Margaret Drabble's heroines. It neatly exemplifies, too, their insoluble problem. The woman undergraduate's interest is divided between her academic work and her feminine destiny, which at the university stage appears as though it will take the conventional social forms. The conflict is between the duty of the self-imposed task and instinct.

The working out of this post-graduate feminine destiny, which may be painful, disillusioning or otherwise unexpected, is a staple ingredient in Margaret Drabble's subject matter (see Chapter 6).

Despite her first in Schools, Sarah does not stay on for research. "You can't be a sexy don," she says, concluding that to succeed in the academic world one would have to play down one's sex appeal, instead of exploiting it. There seems to be general agreement that her judgement is sound. We sympathise with her: fulfilment in a career that demands such suppression can be only half a life for a healthy, attractive girl.

Only one leading character, Rosamund, takes the path Sarah rejects, and stays to work for a Ph.D. Rosamund tells us she is good-looking, and there is confirmation of her claim, in that she gets whistles from men on building sites. But, we read with shock and pity, one of the discoveries she makes when pregnant, and these salutes are no longer forthcoming, is that she had totally depended upon them as "her sole means of sexual gratification."

Such meagre satisfactions would not suit a girl like Sarah, who has a normal endowment of sensuality. But Rosamund, though she insists on her attractiveness, is lopsided in her development, and knows it. Her intellectual success has been achieved at enormous cost, and her capacity for spontaneous enjoyment has been quenched until it is partially released by her love for her baby.

Rosamund overrates the value of her considerable intellectual powers. She cannot bear the thought that she might ever be mistaken, and believes that no foreigner can have quite the same standards of intelligence as products of the English educational system. She refuses to believe that a baby will affect her career:

> I would win, through the evident superiority of my mind: I am industrious as well as equipped.

She feels her future status as Dr Rosamund Stacey will go a long way towards making up for "the anomaly of Octavia's existence," and convinces herself she will be a better parent than any adoptive ones could be.

Her instincts, long thwarted and denied, are here taking over. She muses during her pregnancy that she is becoming aware of facts she had not noticed before, but characteristically submits her new awareness to intellectual analysis. She denies that the irrational is taking its "famed feminine grip" on her and interprets her emotional growth in rationalist terms: "there is nothing logical about ignorance."

Intelligence is Rosamund's criterion for measuring people. She puts down her brother's "curious social revolt" in reverting to the Tory norms of his economic level to his "not being very intelligent." She thinks her sister Beatrice suffers from "a graduate sense of not using her degree."

Reflecting with conscious irony on the puritanism they have both inherited, she thinks that Beatrice's conscience is probably consoled by the unpleasantness of her social life in the Midlands.

Clara, like Simon, finds the climb up the educational ladder a strain: both of them have to become chameleons. Clara in her teens does not care for the available boys: she tries to, hoping that a taste for them, like the taste for "other desirable sophistications of life, such as alcohol and nicotine" can be acquired by hard work. When she finally commits herself to Gabriel Denham, it is because she sees him as a means of self-advancement. She tells him she cannot love: "I am too full of the will to love." Simon's capacity for love, too, has been trampled out in the climb.

In her teens, Clara's learning is "beyond her experience": she imagines the laurel wreaths of poets and emperors as like the grimy suburban foliage of her home town. Jane Gray, similarly, recognises a curlew not from ornithological knowledge, but from poetry she has read. The puritan hard work for self-advancement which drives people up the educational ladder can distort, can cut people off from direct knowledge of nature.

Simon, reflecting that, if his mother had not aspired, she would have sunk or died, acknowledges:

> Oh Christ, it was exhausting, this living on the will, this denial of nature, this unnatural distortion: but if one's nature were harsh, what could one do but deny it, and repudiate it in the hope that something better might thereby be? It was for him that she had hoped, and so on, through the generations.

For R. H. Tawney*

> . . . will is the essence of puritanism, and for the intensification and organisation of will every instrument in the tremendous arsenal of religious fervour is mobilised. The puritan is like a steel spring compressed by an inner force, which shatters every obstacle by its rebound. Sometimes the strain is too tense, and when its imprisoned energy is released, it shatters itself.

Margaret Drabble is more aware than her created characters of the puritan danger of shattering oneself by too great a distortion of the will.

Secondary characters like Sarah's sister Louise and Jane's cousin Lucy don't throw their whole being into university work. They assert their instinctive natures (though Louise later denies hers in

* *Religion and the Rise of Capitalism.*

a loveless marriage) by sleeping around, and don't bother to get high classes in their finals. Leading characters, though, expend strenuous effort at university and do rather well.

Sarah often feels the impulse to tell everyone she has a good degree, which is, as she sees, "a danger signal." To dwell on past triumphs like a high class in one's examinations when one is only moderately successful in one's present career is a desperate over-compensation for current failure.

Asked if she is to become a don's wife, Sarah replies sharply, "No, I'm going to marry a don." She is anxious not to sink her identity in marriage. Emma, refusing to be identified either as an actress (which she is not) or a housewife (which she is) takes pleasure in telling people she used to be a fashion model.

The ability to think in quotations seems to Sarah the only benefit her education has bestowed. She tries, however, to resist talking in them. Here Margaret Drabble accurately as usual reflects the current scene.

People who graduated twenty or thirty years ago luxuriate, if they have read literature, in quoting from it in conversation. For the last decade young graduates have considered this habit pretentious. They consider it as affected as the interim generation of quotation-mongers consider the Edwardian habit of scattering one's talk with phrases in French.

While Sarah is still at Oxford, Louise says, "It gets you a long way . . . writing essays on human nature. . . . You really find a lot out, studying other people's study-bound conceptions of human nature in your own study don't you?"

Sarah replies "crossly," "Yes, I think you do." But Sarah learns that life is not what she had thought it was, when she was still at Oxford.

Emma suffers from the same purposelessness and despair as Sarah, partly because she has not been to university. Her friend Mary Scott went to London and became a teacher: Emma went to Italy and lived in London and did nothing: "our lives had been turned quite neatly upside down."

Emma, fishing bits of soggy wet cotton out of the washing, wonders what her intellectual friends in Rome and London, undergraduates at two universities, would think if they could see her now.

Lost and lonely in Hereford, Emma looks back with regret to her school:

> the only place in my life where I had been fully classified, fully accounted for and fully known.

Sarah, with her first in English, looks back to the university library as a "womb." University work had provided

> a week to find the answer and someone to tell me I was right or wrong.

In those days there had been knowledge to discover: in the world outside that womb it seems not to exist. Emma, with her puritan habit of self-discipline, "keeps in condition," though she doesn't know what for. She reads Italian novels to feed the "munching jaws" of her mind.

Sarah's problem is not solved at the end of the novel: she still does not really know what to do with herself. She has the puritan strenuousness of effort, the puritan restraints of conscience, but lacks the puritan sense of "calling" in its secularised meaning of "vocation."

Her isolation is, though, reduced by closer contact with her sister, and she has learned to take spontaneous enjoyment in life. This means adjusting her expectations downwards, though. She suspects that she must be "so bloody brilliant that everybody else . . . seems to be at half pressure." So she gives up looking for "Dostoevskys in corners" and prefers a good laugh. She wishes she could write a book half as good as Amis's *Lucky Jim*. Louise has learned that middle-class girls are "fools to expect other people to respect the same gods as themselves and E. M. Forster."

Both Sarah with her conventional conscience in conflict with her hunger for success, and Emma with her home-made do-it-yourself code which she as strenuously observes, long to go back to a world of rules, discipline and order. In the real world they find only chaos, which Emma, womanlike, tries to order by "sweeping up a few crumbs."

Clara is spared this crisis: at the end of *Jerusalem the Golden* she is still training as a teacher. Her strains come earlier: she finds it "hard work, the acquiring of opinions." She envies Clelia and Gabriel, who seem to her to have been born with views:

"they had known from infancy which pictures to pin up on their walls."

Her intellectual and social diffidence (both of which she conceals) are inseparable. She has had to grow, painfully, "by will and strain." She knows nothing of the etiquette of meeting performers after poetry readings, yet recognises that compliments are a "duty."

She has a clear vision of other worlds, which keeps her going. In her teens she is excited to think that a Western film can be a classic, and when a boyfriend praises Northam Town Hall (Clara later finds his *mot* in Betjeman), she enjoys imagining situations in which such knowledge might be an asset.

But her intelligence embarrasses her: she wishes she could fail exams like ordinary children, and although her state scholarship cheque speaks to her "industrial heart decisively," she feels she is being paid for being a freak. She never learns to take, as Rosamund does, simple satisfaction in her abilities: she sees them always as a "bargaining power rather than a blessing."

Baffled by the phrase, common in Northam, "I don't know much about it, but I know what I like," Clara arrives independently at Stephen Potter's conclusion that if you don't know much about it then you don't know what you like. "She might have ventured, after hesitation, to prefer Zola to Hugo," but these are her formal subjects of study. Of English literature, which luckier children absorb from their surroundings, she knows little. The skills of poetry readers are to her "as alien . . . as the skills of football players." Told that a glamorous, audible actress is not good, Clara's suspicion that she is a "soft option" is confirmed. "How could anything so pleasant be good?" Excellence is associated, in Clara's mind, with painfully acquired tastes.

Here Margaret Drabble crystallises in dramatic form the conflict of the intelligent grammar school pupil whose home offers no supporting culture. Such people are weaned from what they spontaneously enjoy to acquire an alien set of values. Sometimes they remain stranded, without making it to the distant shores of the alternative culture offered. Or they can be left adrift, like Clara, afraid to like or enjoy anything which has not been sealed with approval by a higher authority.

Clara compensates by seeking information, as Emma compensates for her metaphysical doubts by collecting facts. Hearing of Sebastian Denham, Clara does her homework, looking him up in the Penguin guides: she is ashamed not to have heard of him. Anchorless in the world of culture, she diligently tries to make up her deficiencies. Her true education takes place not at London university, but in the company of the Denham family.

Clara's horizons, though, are limited and at the end of the book she has attained her objectives. Unlike Emma, Sarah and Jane, her expectations are fulfilled.

Emma looks back to her school days, when she used to be ambitious, and when

> the paltry nature of my life at school and home, compared with my vast expectations, reduced me to a state of sleepwalking paralysis.

Jane, though in adulthood she insists that she cares for "nothing much" and that as a child she was "unhopeful," in childhood collected marbles. With them she seemed always on the edge of discovery, "some activity too delightful to bear, and yet I could never quite reach it." She used to play a game of shopping, which seemed to promise " bliss beyond belief," some "violent orgasmic moment . . . where we would *become* adults . . . but the moment never happened."

Jane, who went to Oxford partly through family connexion, "the old stale air of patronage," presumably feels the "pinch, the rub, the cold exposure" when coming back to the outside world. We gather this from her surprise that Lucy does not, after Cambridge where there are eight men to every woman.

It seems that Jane marries almost as soon as she comes down, and although she is described as living with some girls in a flat, we are only told that she does "some undistinguished temporary" job.

University women, in Margaret Drabble's books, are conscious of having achieved, through their own efforts, some degree of academic success, and have longings and expectations, but the problem of what to do with themselves, of how to relate to the world outside the womb, remains. The characters all have to mature, slowly and with difficulty, into the courage to face adult life.

Characters are conscious of their gifts, though only Rosamund has any clear idea what to do with them. And Rosamund's single-mindedness has been achieved at the cost of suppression. It is shaken, but not destroyed, when the experience of motherhood awakens her dormant instincts. Commitment to educational effort, in accordance with the puritan ideal of self-advancement, can necessitate suppression of one's spontaneous impulses. Yet what else are the gifted to do? Emma, having missed out on university, suffers starvation of the "munching jaws" of her mind. The conflict is insoluble. It is Margaret Drabble's achievement to have analysed and dramatised it, as no previous novelist has done. Women, because of the motherhood–career problem, probably suffer from post-graduate malaise even more than do men.

Jane is terrified that she might be uniquely gifted, but she is afraid of being "forever exiled in the painful space between desire and arrival." Her "orgasmic moment" of maturity never arrives: she later adds, "And so it was with sex."

6

Men, women and children

She rose to his requirement, dropped
The playthings of her life
To take the honorable work
Of woman and of wife.

If aught she missed in her new day
Of amplitude or awe,
Or first prospective, or the gold
In using wore away,

It lay unmentioned, as the sea
Develops pearl and weed,
But only to himself is known
The fathoms they abide.
                    Emily Dickinson.

The days are over, thank God, when a woman justifies her existence by marrying.—Sarah, *A Summer Birdcage*.

Time and maternity can so force and violate a personality that it can hardly remember what it was.—Emma, *The Garrick Year*.

All happy families are alike, but an unhappy family is unhappy after its own fashion.—Tolstoy.

There didn't seem to be many female perversions in that book. Perhaps it was because it was old. Perhaps women have developed these things more recently as a result of emancipation.—Jane, *The Waterfall*.

Male readers of Margaret Drabble comment that she reflects very much a woman's world: housework, cooking, breastfeeding, the "indescribable cotton salty hygienic womanly smell of sanitary towels," the "bleeding womb," "swollen aching untouchable breasts," "impacted breast ulcers," the "blue white scars of child-bearing," the "scars and patched wounds of maternity," being "stitched and sewn" and "remade badly," understandable failures with Dutch caps.

The most obvious failure to adjust to the sexual role is Jane's: as a girl, she faints when she reads the instructions on a packet of Tampax. When first married, she tries, puritan fashion, to "obey the rules" and practise contraception, but birth control, taken seriously by her parents' generation, is just a bad joke to her. How can one decide in advance to make love one day and refrain the next, she asks, pleading for spontaneity. Eventually her toddler finds the neglected rubber cap in a drawer and plays with it in his bath until it perishes. Jane is distressed by the routines of prenatal shaving and postnatal examinations, "rubber fingers inside my dead flesh." Phillipa, Gabriel Denham's wife, fails to use her Dutch cap because she is "too narrow." Phillipa, a minor character, is in a state of neurotic withdrawal. This state is made the plight of the narrator of the next novel, *The Waterfall*, in which Jane is always ill at ease with her own body. Like Phillipa, Rosamund and Rose, she picks destructively at furnishings and her own cuticles.

Jane is convinced of the "sexual doom of womanhood, its sad inheritance." Sarah dreads "the embroidery, the children, the sagging mind" and fears all women are doomed. It is Jane who discovers that the thrombotic clot induced by the contraceptive pill is "the price the modern woman must pay for love," while Zola's Nana got the pox.

Jane and Phillipa are mentally ill, but their anxiety about frigidity is shared by Emma and Rosamund, both physically healthy and mentally strong, but sharing a distrust of their own bodies. Emma feels it is only the "physical rubbish" of her, the "blood and skin," which respond to Wyndham in sexual excite-ment. She has the puritan sense that the body is corrupt, and ponders "our tatty sexual decadence."

It is not clear whether Sarah has slept with her Francis or not: it doesn't really matter. Her sister Louise asks Sarah what she thinks it would feel like to be a virgin bride, and Sarah says like

a lamb being led to slaughter. Rosamund becomes an unmarried
mother after one brief encounter, Emma and Rose both sleep with
their husbands before marriage, but this does not make adjustment any easier. Clara, who has been cheerfully promiscuous,
enjoys the secrecy of being mistress to a married man whose wife
refuses him sex. But because of conditioning Clara has a different
set of sexual hang-ups. Not bred to casual embraces, she cannot take them lightly, cannot call anyone "darling." Meeting the
Denhams for the first time she ponders the implications of hand-
holding in their circle. Men find Clara more lavish with acts than
with words, and even then she is the one who offers her cheek
rather than the one who kisses. Jane and Malcolm refrain from
intimacy before marriage and have very little after it.

None of Margaret Drabble's women shares a relaxed and happy
relationship with a man. Rosamund is startled at the lingering
descriptions of sexual ecstasy in her friend Joe's novels. (Margaret
Drabble provides no such descriptions.) Jane achieves sexual
ecstasy in adultery, and when she does, profoundly distrusts it.

Margaret Drabble is interested in the inevitable tensions between men and women. Her male characters are not strongly characterised, but are all different. They are less vivid to us than the
women because, except in the case of Simon (a fully realised and
impressive character), we do not share their thoughts. Only rarely
are the tensions between the sexes resolved.

Sarah reflects, in an image with disturbingly physical under-
tones, that while men are "defined and enclosed," women in order
to live must be "open and raw to all comers." Emma concludes
that she has opened herself to Wyndham either too little or too
much, and had ended up with neither fidelity nor satisfaction.
The problem for women is how to be "open" and yet protect
themselves.

Jane wonders whether she will go mad like Sue Bridehead in
Jude the Obscure. Sue Bridehead is significant, for in his college-
trained teacher Hardy foresaw the conflicts educated women would
suffer: Sue suppresses her instincts for conditioned principles.
Hardy's picture of Sue was prophetic. Her story was strangely re-
enacted in the lives of Maude Gonne and Katherine Mansfield, both
gifted women who found it difficult to adjust to the conflicting
claims of self-fulfilment and marriage. Margaret Drabble's edu-

cated wives inherit this conflict. Emma, intelligent though not a graduate, is delighted to get the job of television newsreader, as this way she can fulfil her "conflicting responsibilities." This way of putting it shows that she feels she has a responsibility to herself, as well as to David and the children.

Emma is afraid of her own immaturity and "inability to grow." She tells her lover, Wyndham,

> I connect love . . . with babies. And being tired. And wanting to go to sleep. And I don't want that, I just want a good time.

She has put in more than three years of "forbearance and patience" with her husband, and her experience of life and maternity has brought disillusion.

She tantalises her lover by withholding herself, so that he tells her she has the "attraction of the difficult," in implicit allusion to Yeats. He tells her: "It makes me feel proud . . . when I get anything out of you." He seems to share the puritan sense of the value of effort, but as when Emma talks about paying her debt to him, the puritan value of fidelity in marriage is not acknowledged, for both are talking of adultery.

The only Margaret Drabble heroine (apart, possibly, from Sarah) who takes sex naturally is Rose. Her nature is distorted by a morbid religiosity, but her instincts assert themselves in her choice of husband, the sexy, dirty, beautiful Christopher, and in her adultery with a foreigner who "smells of railway carriages" and is attractive in some "obscene sexy way"; his skin is "dirty and slippery." This affair occurs because Anton misunderstands Rose when she says she is going to bed. Rose "could never have made much of a virtue of chastity as Noreen did, she was not made of the right kind of flesh or spirit." But Rose's preference for unwashed lovers hints at masochism, a hint reinforced by the information that, divorcing Christopher for cruelty, she did not mention things he had done to her which she had "quite enjoyed at the time." As a girl, Rose has had fantasies of rape, another masochistic symptom, but is not masochist enough to be pleased when Christopher forces his way into her bed after the divorce and translates her youthful fantasies into disagreeable reality.

In her acceptance of sex Rose is atypical of Margaret Drabble's women. Rosamund recalls her physical relationship with George in terms of lips and teeth and naked flesh: "images of fear, not of desire." She believes that an incestuous friendship will outlast love. Jane sees her choice of James, her cousin by marriage, as incest, based on proximity. Gabriel does not deny Clara's suggestion that his family is "rife with incest": Clara says he would have married his sister Clelia if he could. This preference for incest indicates sexual immaturity, a fear of committing oneself to full relationships in the outside world.

This immaturity is betrayed by several female characters in a preference for epicene men. Rosamund, wondering whether her strange attitude to sex is due to the "over-healthy, businesslike attitude" of her family or her intellectual isolation as a child, or a "hatred of being pushed around," chooses George. George wears "quietly effeminate clothes" and his conversation is couched in "camp parlance." Rosamund likes him because alone among her acquaintance he is not entirely obsessed with his soul or his career, but, more significantly:

> We subsided together and lay there quietly. Knowing that he was queer, I was not frightened of him at all . . .

Her motives for letting him seduce her are characteristically complicated.

> I thought it would be good for me . . . I managed to smile bravely, in order not to give offence, despite considerable pain . . .

Jane marries the sexually ambiguous Malcolm, who shows little desire for her before marriage. She accuses him, later, of being homosexual, but he has in fact left her for another woman. Physically, however, he is thin and unmasculine. She thinks she chooses him for social reasons, to escape gentility, but her unwritten message is that she prefers a man who will be sexually undemanding, as she is afraid of all desire and cannot reconcile her flesh and her mind. The split is more or less healed by her affair with James, but she is horrified to find satisfaction "black, addictive, insatiable."

> She had held on, in wise alarm, to her virginity, through marriage, through childbirth . . . pure as a nun, because she had always known it would destroy her, such knowledge.

81

She is convinced (against all psychological probability) that James will hate her for her abandonment and her preceding desire. Her fears are characteristically expressed in religious terms: she has been led to this experience "like a sacrifice."

Emma is afraid of passion because it obscures one's "sense of identity" and this is perhaps the real problem for other heroines. Proud, intelligent and self-conscious, these women have formed such identity as they have achieved by effort, and are afraid to submit to instinct.

Emma has a virile husband, but in a significant dream walks in prelapsarian innocence with Julian, "passionately in love," although she cannot imagine what his "thin girl's body" would feel like, "so different from Wyndham's solid trunk or David's muscular torso." She feels for Julian in her dream "all that I had ever felt for anyone."

Her immaturity is signalled by her preference for rehearsals over performances, for eating three plates of *hors d'œuvres* instead of a main course, and by withholding from her lover any caresses below the waist.

Julian is eventually drowned in the river, having committed suicide from indecision. Emma and David are too strong to follow suit: their marriage is a battle for domination, both are unfaithful, but they end up reconciled.

> I lay . . . saying "I love you, David" not particularly because I meant it or felt it, but because I knew that in view of the facts it must be true. We had too much in common . . . David and I, ever to escape.

Earlier on, she had not much liked the "mess of union." Emma's sin has been not so much her adultery as her failure to love either David or Wyndham truly and generously.

Louise's husband is suspected by Sarah of being "queer" and Louise does not deny it: "I don't know why he's spent so much of his . . . time running after girls." The choice of Louise's heart is John, a handsome, vital actor, but she seeks at first security with an epicene, rich man. At the end of the book she is living with John, finding true maturity when her first, wrong choice rejects her. Living in technical adultery with the man she loves, she restores herself and is even able to offer affection to her sister.

Although Jane and Malcolm destroy each other with nagging and neglect, she acknowledges at the end, "I don't much believe in the sacrament of marriage, but it is to him that I am married, for all that." Malcolm does not carry out his threat to divorce her. Simon recognises that second marriages are built on destruction, on the weeping of infants. Rose does divorce Christopher, but his longing for his children, expressed in a protracted legal battle, drives her to take him back, although at one point she considers "renouncing" them to him. James, too, is fond of children. He first climbs into Jane's bed when she has just given birth, eats the remnants of babyfood which Jane finds disgusting, and nags his wife Lucy to give him more children, although Lucy dislikes having them and they have three already.

Emma, Rosamund and Jane all have sexual difficulties and early resentment of pregnancy: (the usual fears for their figures, no more cinemas, no more possibility of work or freedom: Emma feels pregnancy even robs her of "hope and expectation").

She regards motherhood as "like hay fever or asthma," a complaint which gets no sympathy, but finds it has "infinite compensations."

> I was devoted to Flora . . . what I had dreaded as the blight of my life turned out to be one of its greatest joys.

Wyndham's accusation that the children are all she does love is justified: she resists advances by two men who suggest she ditches the children for them. After the affair is over, Emma reports that Wyndham's new girl looks rather like herself and also seems to live on *hors d'oeuvres*.

> He said he hoped my children were well and that he would never fall in love with a woman with children again.

Emma has never contemplated real irresponsibility: she has only been playing with the idea. She wonders how anybody can maintain a concealed affair when it is impossible to get out of the house for more than five minutes. When Flora falls into the river, Emma unhesitatingly jumps in and fishes her out. She has only to look at Flora to discover where her heart is. It is the "duty" of her visitors to praise Flora's beauty and intelligence.

> Those with children, however unwillingly . . . are in many ways irrevocably cut off from those without, and David and I watched Flora pursuing her peas with a unity of enthusiastic tenderness that we could not feel for anything else.

Jane finds childbirth terrifying, and considers a stoic calm the only way of enduring its universal trials. She reflects on the injustice of afterpains, which herald no second birth, but finds that the pangs, "lightly undertaken and bitterly endured," are soon forgotten. Lacking confidence in herself, she finds her own beauty a "menace and a guilt and a burden" and distrusts her body: she is amazed that she can give birth so easily. She looks to children and their mothers for redemption:

> . . . seeing any mother show concern for her children, "Oh, redeem yourselves for me, she would cry to herself: let me redeem myself, in you."

Jane has given suck and feels as though the baby were "pulling at her guts." This is a common experience, which many women readers will recognise and share. But Jane's emotional reaction is unusual, because of her neurosis:

> It seemed strange . . . that so much natural instinctive force could flow through such a medium as herself, a woman so frail and flawed. She wondered why her own frailty did not interrupt the process, did not keep the milk from the child, or the child from the light.

Even breastfeeding for Jane is associated with feelings of guilt and inadequacy. "Frailty" for her is both physical and moral. She is preoccupied with liquidity, afraid of the liquids within "our stiff bodies." When she finds sexual fulfilment with James, she weeps in joy and amazement at such a beautiful experience.

> That a desire so primitive could flow through her, like milk, astonished her.

Sexual fulfilment, for Jane, is seen in an image of its result: maternity and lactation. The maternal impulse in Jane, as in Rosamund and Emma, seems stronger and less complicated than sexual desire.

Clara, back at home when her mother lies dying, wants to make herself a cup of Ovaltine. But there is no milk in the house. Neither Clara's mother nor her home have given her any spiritual or intellectual nourishment and Mrs Maugham has been deficient in the "milk of human kindness."

Jane and Rose both breastfeed. Emma gives it up because her breasts are too big (and Wyndham is disappointed by the consequent shrinkage). Rosamund gives it up, because it is inconvenient, and because she lacks confidence in her own body.

Rosamund shows characteristic confusion, despite a high degree of verbal clarity, about breastfeeding, which she gives up because she dislikes it. Self-distrusting in all matters save intellectual ones,

> despite evidence to the contrary, I could never believe there was anything there, that the baby was really getting anything at all to drink . . . unnatural I suppose . . . but . . . I was glad I had an alternative. Anyway, only posh middle-class mothers nurse these days, on principle, and I don't believe in principle. I believe in instinct, on principle.

This confusion (depicted with marvellous wit and skill by Margaret Drabble) expresses and dramatises Rosamund's fundamental difficulties in life. She asserts a belief in instinct, a belief we have seen she cannot possibly attain. She denies her ingrained belief in principle, yet uses the key notion of "principle" to justify to herself the freedom she is willing herself into believing in.

Here is puritan conditioning with a vengeance, in that she associates "instinct" with what many people would call a denial of it: the refusal to breastfeed. One suspects she associates this refusal with "instinct," wild and ungoverned, because she finds this refusal pleasurable, a self-indulgence.

She probably dislikes breastfeeding because it is a process, like pregnancy and childbirth, where the body takes over, subject to no control by the mind. Her inability to believe that her breasts hold any nourishment may be a rationalisation of such reluctance to submit to an animal function. It certainly shows her lack of any real confidence, despite her protestations, in her own body, and her excessive intellectualism. This reliance on the intellect alone makes her so one-sided, an asexual mother.

After expecting so little, the beauty of her baby is an amazing joy. Like Jane, she reflects on the speed with which the pains are forgotten, but characteristically she distrusts nature: it is one of its

> horrible tricks to make one forget instantly all that one had feared and suffered, presumably so that one will carry on gaily with the next.

Rosamund even takes it for granted that she should know better than the nurses about the frequency of her contractions. Here for the first time her arrogance and her instincts are reconciled, as she is right about her own body and the baby's imminence. Instinct has already asserted itself in her irrational pride in her own fertility. Her "narrow pelvis" is examined by doctors before the birth

> like a corpse examined by budding pathologists for the cause of death. But I was not dead, I was alive twice over.

Having no husband, she shoulders her responsibilities single-handed.

> It was no longer a question of what I wanted: this time there would be somebody else involved. Life would never be a simple question of self-denial again.

She smocks dresses for Octavia, thus with puritanical thrift avoiding the waste of an accomplishment.

Becoming self-sufficient, after the birth she develops no interest in men; meeting George, she is

> safely back in my old role, the girl with alternating lovers, the girl with stray babies, the girl who does what she wants and does not suffer for it.

This of course is far from the truth of Rosamund's experience, but this is the front her puritan stoicism presents to the world. She pretends to have embraced the permissive values of her generation, while remaining a rigid Victorian at heart. She longs to throw herself on her knees in front of George,

> to beseech from him his affection, his tolerance, his pity, any-thing that would keep him there with me, and save me from being so much alone with my income tax forms.

The inclusion of income tax forms, which at first reading makes us smile at their conjunction with elevated emotions, shows us Margaret Drabble's poise as a writer. At second reading one sees that concrete things are as important in relationships as abstract ones.

But Rosamund's stubborn independence finally rejects George: she does not want him in her bed any more, and denies him knowledge of his paternity. The ultimate commitment to community, which she has been approaching through her baby, is beyond her.

The Denhams, who represent spiritual bounty, have five children. Clelia, the daughter who cannot bring herself to leave home, is also maternal. She takes care of a friend's baby, whose mother has run away. Martin, the baby's father, says, "The maternal impulse seems to run riot in your family, doesn't it?"

Only Julie, Simon's greedy and unhappy wife, "looks maternal without liking children." Her husband thinks she really wants fun, youth, friends instead, as such an unsatisfied woman has nothing left over for children. But even this is a partial judgement, not final:

> He wronged her in his mind, wilfully. It gave him some malicious satisfaction.

No mother in Margaret Drabble's books would agree with Simon's conviction that it is dreadful that children are born of two parents with equal claims, that they do not spring fully grown from the brain, as Athene did from that of Zeus. Simon is thinking of the struggle between Rose and Christopher over their children, and muses that man is "condemned for survival to partition." This is a characteristic Margaret Drabble play on words: partition can mean division, as when the amoeba reproduces itself by splitting, or distribution into shares. She is probably thinking, too, of "parturition." In law, partition means a division of property. All these meanings are present in Simon's thoughts as presented to us. Simon is thinking of the children as property their parents are squabbling over.

But it is in motherhood that Margaret Drabble's clever women, despite difficulties arising from distrust of their own bodies and resentments about loss of freedom, move towards their true identities.

Drabble heroines (except for Clara, who does not give birth, and Rose, who as we have seen has a different emotional make up from the self-conscious intellectuals) characteristically combine sexual frigidity with passionate maternal feeling.*

Yet in each case, she makes this fear and dislike of sex consistent in terms of each character as conceived and developed. Emma's frigidity is due to her self-centredness, which she later outgrows. Rosamund's is due to her background and confirmed by her chosen lifestyle, which we recognise (although she does not) to have been evasive and self-protective. Jane's is even better delineated than Rosamund's: it is graphically presented as part of her neurosis. Jane's neurosis, growing from her nurture, is marvellously depicted, and we feel with her at every step of her partial recovery.

One's initial impatience with such foolishness on the part of the heroines diminishes, too, when one considers Margaret Drabble's oeuvre as a whole. In it we see the pattern underlying all her work, the pull of instinct against the puritan restraints which characters have internalised.

Maternal love and joy welling up in these women is purified for them, as sexual love is not, by the knowledge that the pleasures of motherhood demand commitment to the puritan virtues of self-sacrifice and responsibility. Yet even commitment to motherhood can represent an evasion: Jane and Rosamund, who share the puritan fear of submitting to judgement, express relief that their children are too young to judge them.

There is no instance, among Margaret Drabble's main characters, those whose thoughts we are allowed to share, of a mother rejecting her child, unable to love it.

Only Mrs Sharkey's Eileen, Rose's neighbour, deserts her baby, dropping it in her mother's lap. Poor Eileen enjoys the vicarious glamour of Rose's newspaper notoriety, and at nineteen, having had a baby by a married man, sets off for the bedding factory. Rose thinks Eileen is finished, excluded forever from her hopes.

---

* Professor Ivor Mills, of Addenbrooke's Hospital, Cambridge, tells me this is an increasingly common problem among intelligent, educated women.

. . . the gulf between her reality and her aspirations was total and would remain so. . . . Gone was Eileen, the wicked lady, driving round in taxis, wearing fur coats, drinking cocktails: gone was Eileen the make-up girl with false eyelashes and a pink overall: gone was Eileen the garage man's girl, taking trips up the motorway in a fast car.

But later Eileen goes "even more to the bad"; she leaves the bedding factory and takes up with a gang of Hell's Angels. Rose finds this exhilarating, although she doesn't know why. But we do. Rose has found no satisfaction nor comfort in doing her duty, sharing her children with her husband: she longs for the peace of her withdrawn days. Eileen, unencumbered by puritan ethics or the gloomy teachings of Evangelicals, is asserting her capacity for spontaneous enjoyment.

7

Love, salvation, survival

The novel, then, is a perpetual quest for reality, the field of its research being always the social world, the material of analysis being always manners as the indication of a direction of man's soul.—Lionel Trilling.

You've got no idea, said Christopher, how absolutely wicked and selfish people are when they get hold of this idea of being good. —*The Needle's Eye.*

And lo! Ben Adhem's name led all the rest.—Leigh Hunt.

A perpetual winter was what he expected: he would he felt, experience no surprise should, one spring, the trees refuse to bud, and the flowers to blossom. Why should those branches not remain forever bare, the earth forever hard and inhospitable? By what grace did these green hopes and gentle exhalations perpetually recur?

In *The Needle's Eye* we find vegetation imagery linked explicitly with hope and renewal, a traditional enough association. More surprising, but characteristic, is the mention in the passage of "grace," a key concept in Margaret Drabble's work.

Simon, the embittered pessimist who "lacks charity" and "cannot love," is astonished by the mildness of the air. Simon's intimations of hope are later justified, although for a while his spirit (in the traditional image of a bird)

would hunch its feathered bony shoulders and grip its branch, and fold itself up and shrink within itself, until it could no longer brush against the net . . . no longer tangle itself, painfully, in the surrounding circumstantial mesh.

For Simon, there is no light,

> or none that man might enter: he could create for himself an
> ordered darkness, an equality of misery, a justice in the sharing
> of darkness, his own hole, by right, in the darkness, and his sense
> of light, his illuminations, were an evolutionary freak, an artificial
> glow that had etiolated him into hopeless pale unnatural under-
> ground deformities, a light misreflected through some unintended
> chink, too far away for such a low creature ever to reach it and
> flourish by it. He might as well lose his eyes, man.

This evolutionary image has strong religious overtones. Simon
sees in life's continuity only

> a ghastly chain of reiterated disillusions, in which each generation
> discovers new impossibility, the more miserably because it had
> been given to hope for more.

But on meeting Rose, Simon's despair gives way to hope, although
at first he does not recognise it as such. They discuss Simon's
lack of charity. He admits to a strong sense of obligation, but
says he has found it "destructive of the emotions." He says to
her:

> I am glad you can enjoy going shopping and taking advantage
> of cut price offers. I wish that I too could arrive at such a state
> of grace.

Simon's first impression of Rose is of

> age and softness, authentic, as ancient frescoes look in churches,
> frescoes which in their very dimness offer a promise of truth that
> a more brilliant (however beautiful) restoration denies.

The back of Rose's hand is "brown and slightly crazed like an
old earthernware pot." Rose, in her authenticity, her worn surfaces, represents a survival of ancient religious truth. Visiting a
church with his daughter, Simon sees an inscription on the
wall: "They sorrow not as those that have no hope" and he
imagines this represents his own state of mind. He buys Kate
a postcard, a "crudely tinted thing with a falsely smiling sky
and a floral graveyard." She is astonished that she is trusted to
pay, and is "amazed at the church's faith" that she will. Simon
later decides that he has "hopes for Kate," the next generation:
she is a "survivor."

Simon continues to be interested in Rose: he believes she confers a special "light," an especial "favour."

> He thought he understood her. He wished to understand. Such a modicum of goodwill (for so he thought it) was nothing less than a rebirth in his nature.

An unbeliever, Simon has had a religious experience: he has found rebirth and some measure of hope in human love, an image of the divine (marked by the comparison of Rose to an old church fresco) and the hope and innocence of a human child, "amazed at the church's faith." Simon is on the way to being healed. His cure is associated with nature, both by the greenery which is a "perpetual exhalation" and the natural cure of a verruca, which he has attempted to hack away from his foot. We remember that his agonised aspiration has been "a denial of nature," a "distortion of the will."

The word "grace" can be used in popular or in technical theological senses. It is unlikely that Margaret Drabble has in mind "habitual, sanctifying" or "providential" grace as defined by the *Oxford Dictionary of the Christian Church*, and conveyed by the sacraments. The sacraments are mentioned only twice in her six books. Jane does "not much believe in the sacrament of marriage." Sarah, told of her brother-in-law Stephen's High Church leanings, replies that Anglicanism is "rich and respectable." She can't see Stephen believing in anything "ridiculous, like God." She imagines Stephen more likely to believe in "something good, solid and social, like the sacrament of marriage instead."

For Sarah, the sacraments have no transcendental value: they are "good, solid and social." She is within the nonconformist tradition, in which the sacraments are no guarantee of salvation. She believes that people cannot be changed:

> they can only be saved or enlightened or renewed, one by one, which is a different thing, and not one that can be affected by legislation.

Salvation, enlightenment, renewal: the vocabulary is that of nonconformist theology, in accordance with Wesley's doctrine that even in this life it is possible to attain freedom from sin by spiritual transformation. Hamlyn's dictionary definition of grace is: "the influence of God . . . to regenerate or strengthen."

In the context of Margaret Drabble's work, "grace" is partially redefined. It seems to mean for her the strengthening power of regeneration, "green hopes and gentle exhalations," in harmony with nature. This harmony with nature is always related to, indeed achieved through, human love. For Margaret Drabble, grace can come to the human soul only when it comes into relationship with others. She does not accept that to win all, one must renounce all. Nor would she accept Weber's definition of grace as understood by Protestants: "Grace, common to all denominations, marks off the possessor from the degradations of the flesh, from the world." Margaret Drabble makes her character, Jane, speak the truth when she feels "her mind and her flesh must meet or die." Through love we come into relationship with the human community and the natural world; life's apparent bleakness can be brightened with "green hopes."

There are hints that Simon and Emma have "prevenient grace" working in them. According to the *OED*, prevenient grace is

> the grace of God which precedes repentance and conversion, predisposing the heart to seek God previous to any desire or motion on the part of the recipient. One can have prevenient grace without knowing it.

Emma asserts several times her belief in providence; Simon is told by Rose that he does care for what is right, and his verruca would probably have healed "in the course of nature." In other words, providence, through nature, would be taking its course without his knowing or doing anything about it. Simon knows what is wrong with him, "but it altered nothing, such knowledge." The intellect alone is no guide: change must come from the heart.

Rose, like Simon, seeks for grace, but her state of soul is more complicated. She hopes she is already in a state of grace, finds an "inexplicable grace" in living withdrawn from society, "like a nun in an enclosed order." Neither the puritan tradition nor Margaret Drabble sees much value in a monastic life. Weber says of the puritans: "The religious life of the saints was lived within the world and its institutions."

When Rose responds to Christopher's love for their children by going back into family life, into society, she looks back with regret. Her withdrawn days, she thinks, had been

> endowed with a spiritual calm it had been a crime to lose. And now she lived in dispute and squalor, for the sake of charity and love. She had ruined her nature against her judgement, for Christopher's sake, for the children's sake . . . the price she had to pay was . . . her own living death . . . her own lapsing from grace, as heaven (where only those souls may enter) was taken slowly from her, as its bright gleams faded. Oh, she knew it had been narrow, her conception of grace, it had been solitary . . . it had been without community.

The last admission gives the clue to moral judgement: Rose's conception of grace had been too narrow; it "had lacked community," and was therefore invalid. Although Rose has considered herself "grossly defective," she considered her defects her "virtues, her faith, her way of life." Forced to take the children on alone, she "had strengthened herself on those hard years, she had developed the muscle to deal with them." Rose has lived on her puritan will, but is then called on to sacrifice her vision of heaven for "charity and love."

The question as to whether she had "ruined her own nature" is not easy, but the image of the pressed flowers (see Chapter 10) suggests that Rose's view of her own nature is mistaken. It was her nature which made her choose her "sexy and undeniable" husband, not the overlay of her grim Evangelical life-denying nurture. Rose is surely as mistaken in her eventual view as she was when signing the cheque for twenty thousand pounds, making a grand gesture of renunciation. As Simon tells her, "You can't get rid of it, grace or riches . . . they increase and multiply." Rose almost certainly has grace without knowing it, like her son Konstantin, although she "did not forgive herself." While the two younger children are "redeemed" by free, unmerited love on Rose's part, paralleling the grace of God, Konstantin is justified by his acts. Rose herself is in all probability redeemed, too, although she feels she has lost faith. Her theological position, at the end of the book, is a "neurotic heroic nonchalance." She never fights free of this neurosis, so her judgements on her own situation are likely to continue to be mistaken.

Rose's husband, Christopher, who is interested in "money, and power, and emotion and love" is wiser. Like another heiress, Asta Allmers in Ibsen's *Little Eyolf*, which like *The Needle's Eye* deals with parental responsibility, Rose inherits vast forests. Her acres of fir trees in Norfolk will be replanted by the Forestry Commission: care by a government body representing the community will ensure their renewal.

Rose's forests have a life-giving potential: her wealth could, and should, be rightly used. At the end of the book, the imagery of forests and the money they represent for Rose are brought together. Simon reflects on Christopher's business skills:

> money coursing like sap through the veins of England . . . Christopher managed to transform it into a moonlight jungle.

Christopher, in using the gifts of this world to their best advantage, is not distorting nature, as Simon has had to in order to climb, and as Rose has done with her own character. Christopher's redeeming involvement is wiser than Rose's retreat, and Rose's conviction that grace came from living alone is placed for us as a delusion.

Like Rose, Jane is mentally unbalanced. Denying any sort of religious faith, she uses constantly the language of Calvinist theology: election, damnation; she is preoccupied with the corruption of the flesh. Describing her return to comparative health through James, she says it was a "miracle," that she received "grace."

> Grace and miracles. I don't much care for my terminology.

To the end she is not clear whether James, in loving her and bringing her the "grace" of human, sexual love, has damned her for her sin of adultery. The decision to write a fictional account of her experiences marks her new power to act, released by James.

> I will invent a morality that condones me. Though by doing so, I risk condemning all that I have been.

Her brave intentions are not carried out: she finds it impossible to invent a morality that condones her and remains in a state of confusion. She is never sure what "grace" means to her, and the word shifts its meaning in different contexts within her book. She thinks she should have had the grace to die in the car crash, yet grace is also associated in her mind with survival, for she is glad that James has the grace to drive carefully.

After the accident she degrades his "easy grace" into mere grace of body and small services like changing electric plugs, "acts of simulated grace." But as she later admits, the grace he brought her was the real thing. She has submitted, at the beginning of the book, "graciously" to childbirth, her "deliverance." Here the physical and the religious are linked by the double meaning of "deliverance" and her deliverance from frigidity and isolation in James's arms makes the same connexion, mingling the sexual and the religious into harmony:

> She gave a strange sobbing cry of rebirth. A woman delivered. She was his offspring, as he, lying there between her legs, had been hers.

For a while she sees her relationship with James as her "sexual salvation" but repudiates this view for a while after the accident, "a judgement on them both." Later she recognises that although there was corruption in their love, it helped and healed her. Nothing is perfect, nothing uncomplicated, she discovers. There are no simple rules of right and wrong.

Until James frees her, she is terrified of love.

> To experience love without pain, without terror and without danger, seemed beyond the realm of human possibility. Human contact seemed to her so frail a thing. . . .

So Jane chooses to isolate herself, "like a nun." The relevance of Kierkegaard's *Journals* to her state has already been noted. SK believes, like Jane, that his melancholy is "an inheritance," like her he has a "discord between the psychical and the physical," like her, he sees himself as "a sacrifice," like her, he is preoccupied with his vocation as a writer. For SK, "self-denial" is "the whole point of Christianity" and he considers the foremost duty of Christians "to return to the monastery from which Luther broke away." He wrote in 1850:

> People will make it appear that I wanted to introduce pietism, little pusillanimous self-abnegations in matters of no consequence.

Jane writes of her "futile renunciations," her "abnegations," her acts of self-sacrifice which she comes to realise she made because she is afraid to admit how much she really wants in life. Like Kierkegaard, Jane chooses isolation in the search for "innocence." But SK rejected human, sexual love, and refused to marry Regine Olsen.

SK tried to win all by renouncing all, and so does Jane. But Margaret Drabble rejects this puritanical solution to the problems of grace and salvation. For her, grace comes through involvement in society, through love of one's fellow men, as does the recognised cure for schizoid disturbance.

While James is away, Jane finds in herself the courage to leave the house, and takes the children to the zoo. She thus involves herself once more with the natural world, even though the animals lead a confined life as do human beings. She finds in Guy, the gorilla, as many have done, an image of her own human confinement and boredom. It is a relief to her to watch the "soulless fishes, ignorantly, happily unaware of their glass confines." But the aquarium windows are "illuminated" and, looking at them, so (metaphorically) is Jane. Walking past, she realises that time will pass, that she can neither stop nor hasten it: "I was through, it would be better, it could not get worse."

After the accident, she realises that all her pride in not having

> had been nothing but a defence against not being given . . . when offered the chance of salvation, I had taken it: I had not cared who should drown, so long as I should reach the land.

Our judgement is that though Jane committed, technically, a social sin in committing adultery with James, yet by involving her once more with the community, through human love, her "sin" was paradoxically her salvation. (Even socially, there is some mitigation in that she is "not the first" as Lucy tells her, and Lucy herself is unfaithful to James.) But Jane, who has feared human nature, and particularly her own, finds in the thawing of her own frozen sexuality the power of love, of harmony, of reconciliation with nature and with human society. In asserting herself to "reach the land" she has recovered her instinct for life, for survival. Her intimation, which she can never confidently confirm, that she has received grace, is surely an illumination of truth. All this belies her conviction, at the time of the car accident, that human love had been an "unworthy object" of faith.

Like Rosamund, Jane admires selfishness, having been brought up to be reticent and undemanding. But Rosamund changes in other ways, too:

> I had always felt for others in theory and pitied the blows of fate and circumstance under which they suffered; but now, myself no longer free, myself suffering, I may say that I felt it in my heart.

As we have seen, Rosamund is never completely redeemed. But she has developed. She now "weeps daily" for some reason or other. She has been, without realising it, hard-hearted, but the common human experience of motherhood and her consequent involvement with other mothers has softened her heart. Rosamund remains agnostic, and rarely uses religious terminology, but she experiences the true moment of conversion, when grace descends.

In the words of Ezekiel (*Authorised version*, Ezekiel, xi, 19), echoed in that key document of puritanism, the document of the Westminster conference of 1647, God promised to those he is to save to "take the stony heart out of their flesh and . . . give them an heart of flesh."

Emma's heart, too, is softened, and she weeps in her new recognition of the truth of Wordsworth, glad to be no longer ignorant.

Gabriel's wife Phillipa weeps for the injustices of the world, and for herself, but her "social conscience" does not propel her towards action of any kind. She neglects her home, husband and children, in a state of agonised withdrawal, like Jane's. She does not allow her husband to make love to her: her tears are no evidence of grace, in Margaret Drabble's created world, since Phillipa can relate to nobody. She has no love to share or give.

But neither can Clara bring Gabriel love. She says, "There is no love in me, I am too full of the will to love." Clara's puritan will militates against the freedom of love. In a phrase which characteristically and neatly fuses the social and the spiritual, the author says:

> . . . she had not been taught to love, she had lacked those expensive, private lessons.

Yet even Clara comes to recognise love as a reality. Going home to visit her dying mother, she overhears two local women talking, looking not unlike her own mother.

> From them seemed to pour such fountains of innocent, lovely, generous solicitude that Clara . . . wondered if her whole vision of Northam might not after all have been a nightmare, and the whole city might have been filled with warm preoccupations, a whole kind city shut to her alone, distorted in her eyes alone. And she felt once more charitably towards herself, that she had no wish to hate; she had merely wanted to live.

Although Clara never achieves a large measure of spiritual growth, she has her moment of enlightenment, and "feels charitably." She has been justified in fulfilling the demands of her own nature, her instinct to live, against the intellectual and spiritual death of her mother's world. Clara is largely redeemed in that she has lived in accordance with her own nature, used her talents, instead of wasting them as her mother has done.

Watching her dying mother, Clara sees that "as she had always known understanding is never anything but fitful." Clara is thinking of her mother's state of consciousness, but on another level her thoughts are the author's ontological statement.

Margaret Drabble's sane characters are not concerned with religious visions. The two unstable ones, Rose and Jane, are. Rose relies for understanding of life on her visions. As a child, she and her friend Joyce have a favourite word, "yonder."

> Neither of them knew what it meant, but . . . the word would evoke a place of such mystic and visionary loveliness, a thin aspiring castle on the brow of a green hill, a tower above the raging sea, a heavenly city.

Living in her squalid house, with fleas, holes in the walls, cold, where neighbouring pensioners buy single eggs, Rose keeps her vision.

> . . . there loomed a shadowy edifice, an inhabited house, a hope for the future: she trembled, she flinched, but she persevered, she had faith, she built up brick by brick the holy city of her childhood, the holy city in the shape of that patched, subsiding house. But her friends, or such friends as continued, through loyalty or

love or curiosity or desire for profit to make the long journey, continued to think she was mad. Hardly a gleam of her vision reached them.

But Rose's vision, as we shall see (Chapters 10 and 11) was delusory: her friends are right, and she would have been wiser to invest her vision in them as a means to salvation.

Jane longs for visionary gleams, but they do not come. When James is away with his family,

> time had stuck. One hears of the eternity of delight experienced by saints and visionaries: I would swear that I had experienced an eternity of nothingness.

When the crash occurs, Jane feels cheated because she gets no personal message from God, whose existence she has denied. (Jane, Rosamund and Simon all pray in desperation to the God they intellectually deny.)

> I had always cherished the faith that at the moment of death I would be immeasurably illumined . . . and I sat there cheated . . . I had believed in the significance of life and . . . God had no right to deny me the white lights that I had hoped for. . . .
>
> But then, I did not die. The moment had been false, a false warning. God had hidden his face for some later unveiling, perhaps.

Jane thinks herself humble, but her estimate of her "appalling faith," her "invincible arrogance" about her poetic gift has religious dimensions, too. She who said there was no sense, no revelation to be hoped for, finds in a moment of crisis that she believes it probable that God will unveil himself to her. It is orthodox Christian doctrine that personal messages from God can only be received by those in a state of grace. This is one of the reasons why Jane is in doubt whether James brought her grace or not. As we have seen, in human terms he did.

Later, when she and James laugh at her "foolish expectation," she always looks anxiously over her shoulder and crosses her fingers lest she should be struck down.

Jane believes in predestination.

> Perhaps I could take a religion that denied freewill, that placed God in his true place . . . himself subject, as Zeus was, to necessity. Necessity is my God.

Later on she realises she was self-deceived in her belief that necessity rules. She is concerned with fate and necessity, but this is not merely the religious problem of election to salvation or damnation, but a symptom of her dislocation, as it extends to trivial everyday matters. Later she admits that she had mistaken inertia for submission to necessity, and admits that she chose James of her own free will.

Jane and Rose, the characters in danger of mental disequilibrium, are the only two seriously to believe in predestination, or even to fear it might be true.

Jane's confusion is demonstrated on the first page:

> There was something sacred in her fate that she dared not countermand by effort. . . .

Later she says:

> In seeking to avoid my fate, like Oedipus, I had met it. In seeking to avoid the sin of treachery, I had embraced it . . . those sick withdrawals had been nothing more than the sighs by which I summoned James to my side. In presenting myself . . . as a woman on the verge of collapse . . . I had been lying.

But we know that she was not lying: her expressions, images, vocabulary, were all indications of her disturbed state. She is once more seeking to cleanse herself of guilt by refusing to admit that she has been mentally ill. She feels that her illness itself is a sin, deserving punishment: that she deserves "whatever bad things come my way," as a penalty for being neurotic. She is trying to overcompensate for her "sin" with James by taking more than her full share of responsibility, when previously she had refused to admit she had any choice at all. But we, the readers, have evidence in her pages that her agony was real, and that Jane's conviction of fate and predestination was part of her dislocation.

Rose, too, is schizoid for part of the time. When she is terrified that Christopher will take the children from her, she sees herself as split in two. She, too, has fears about predestination. Even when she has won through to "neurotic heroic nonchalance" she decides:

> Razors cut, Christ was crucified, man was wicked, Hell was open. It is even true, thought Rose, ruefully . . . that wet grass

gives one rheumatism . . . it being so what can I do to be saved?
She smiled even, visibly, as the words came into her head . . . she
had so long ago abandoned hope of salvation through faith or . . .
works.

She has never been sure whether her visions come from God or the
devil, but like Jane has a magical belief in the sacredness of her
own fate.

She sees herself as chosen to sacrifice her children and go to
Africa, "that hideous dark misery", as her only chance to appease
God. She feels that her refusal to believe that she was damned
from birth is "against the current," thereby implying that she
does, at bottom, believe in her own damnation.

Sitting over her coffee, she imagines that God has always
demanded sacrifices.

> He demanded Isaac. On the hilltop, the innocent. He shall have
> my children. . . . Oh God, oh God, she prayed, release me, be
> merciful, send me an angel with a sword, tell me what I must do
> . . . take away your message.

But God only sends her another Biblical tag, inculcated by
Noreen, leading to "the desert." The image of the desert runs
through the book: Rose lives in an "industrial desert," Uhujudiana
is a desert of dry, cracked mud and Rose and Simon are threatened
with spiritual aridity, the desert of the anguished soul. The message Rose receives is a hard one:

> If ye will not give up wife and mother and children to follow
> me, he said . . . cruelly, ye shall in nowise enter into the kingdom
> of heaven.

God sent an angel with a sword to countermand the sacrifice of
Isaac when Abraham had showed he was willing to obey God's
command. But no angel appears to Rose. Finally she decides she
ought to see a psychiatrist (though she does not do so). She
has realised that giving up her children is merely "the most
horrible renunciation your mind can conceive. It's silly, it's pointless." After arguing some more with her *alter ego*, she recovers
sanity in constructive action: she decides to collect the children
from school. Her children are here and throughout the book
her means to salvation.

Simon too believes in a secular form of the doctrine of predestination, in

> hereditary woe . . . layers and layers of suffering handed down, worse than anything Freud ever proposed in the way of predestination.

For him, the hundred and thirty-seventh psalm, about how the sins of the fathers shall be visited on the children and that the brains of one's enemies shall be dashed upon the rocks (*sic*), is wicked—but true. He thinks, too, of Ezekiel: "the fathers have eaten sour grapes, and the children's teeth are set on edge."

Simon forgets that in Ezekiel (xviii, 3, 4):

> God reproveth the unjust parable of the sour grapes

and

> As I live, saith the Lord God, ye shall not have any more to use this proverb in Israel. Behold, all souls are mine . . .

Later God promises that the son who sees

> all his father's sins which he hath done, and considereth and doeth not such like . . . that . . . hath executed my judgements, hath walked in my statutes; he shall not die for the iniquity of his father, he shall surely live.

(Ezekiel, xviii, 14–17). Simon denies freewill: he sees in Rose's family garden, with its formal design, only "the intolerable pretensions of those who think themselves free to operate."

Jane, in a state of spiritual desolation like Simon and Rose, also believes in hereditary woe. She believes that her children have "an inheritance of afflictions," she does not know how to break "the fatal hereditary chain." She says she is "like my generation, corrupt," but does not mean merely her age-group. She is thinking of the original sin in which man is born, in which man is conceived. "Generation" or breeding is for Jane corrupt, and so (until she is released from her frigidity) is sex. She is afraid of "human nature." She speaks of herself repeatedly as a sacrificial victim, characteristically, in accordance with her schizoid state, turning her aggression upon herself.

Rosamund, too, thinks God might take Octavia as a sacrifice, taking vengeance on Rosamund by the baby's death. She even hopes, for five minutes, that Octavia might die "and so relieve me from the corruption and fatality of love."

In seeing love as "corrupt" and "fatal," Jane and Rose are misguided. In the visions they share with Simon of a jealous God, demanding sacrifice, they are unable to move further forward than the Old Testament (deeply influential among nonconformist sects).

They forget that, according to the New Testament, Christ is "the propitiation for all our sins" (1 John, ii, 1) and that the message of Christianity is not vengeance, but love.

Their terrors are morbid and a measure of the distance between these individuals and their reconciliation with their true natures in health and love. Clara's escape to Paris is described in terms of election, "the one white soul" flying outwards, though there is no evidence that Clara's concern with election is other than secular. But she shares a superstitious conviction with Jane that by wishing another person dead, she has killed. Feeling guilty about her mother's fatal illness, Clara feels "the hard and narrow clutch of retribution" and sees herself as "a victim . . . a sacrifice." This is, though, before she is reconciled to Northam. She has merely reverted, temporarily to the childish stage described by Freud, when one believes in "the omnipotence of thought."

Convictions of predestination are linked, then, in Margaret Drabble's world, with subjectivity and mental disturbance, not with objectivity or truth.

Like Milton's fallen angels, Margaret Drabble's characters talk

> Of providence, Foreknowledge, will and fate,
> Fixt fate, free will, foreknowledge absolute.

Like the fallen angels, they find "no end, in wandring mazes lost." The word "conjunction" is a favourite of the author's, with its double meaning of "meeting" and "astrological fate." Emma believes in coincidence, as well as in providence. All the characters ponder accidents and disasters. Rose has decided (literally) to "dig her garden." Rosamund, quoting Voltaire, says, *"Il faut culti-ver son jardin"* (sic). But Candide's solution to the problems of life is not Margaret Drabble's.

Metaphysical speculation notably takes place while characters are eating: Simon, after deciding that man "might as well lose his eyes," cuts himself a slice of Gruyère; Rose's decision that she is "mad" to think of sacrificing her children comes while she has "a mouthful of lettuce"; Jane and Lucy wonder why anybody does anything and decide that life is unnecessary while Lucy spreads butter on toast for them both, thus denying by her actions their intellectual conviction.

Sarah says,

> Only when one has got everything in this life, when one is eaten up with physical joy and the extreme, extending marvel of existing, can I trust myself on the subject of the soul.

Sarah is healthier, physically and mentally, than Rose or Jane. She and her sister are described by John as both being "hard as nails." Such hardness can be a virtue in the fight for survival. Sarah once, she says, saw a television programme about schizophrenic children:

> the psychiatrist kept insisting that the condition was rare and biochemical, but it seemed oddly metaphysical to me. . . . The human mind is not a delicate plant, I thought: on the contrary, it will survive almost anything.

Emma and Sophy are both "excellent examples of resilience." At home after a party, Emma asks David whether he meant it when he said that, acting, he just worked at being himself. This question, ostensibly about work, is also about being. David, with all his extravagance and violence, is at one with life in a way Emma at the beginning is not: his salvation is his work as an artist. His answer, like her question, embraces both his work and the existential dimension:

> "What else can I do?" he said. . . . "If I don't be what I am, then I'm not being anything. And if what I am isn't good enough, then I'd better find out . . . I don't want just to get by."

In seeking to find out what he is, David is working in harmony with his own nature. Like the other actor, John in *A Summer Birdcage*, David has superabundant vitality, life in excess.

Comparing herself with Sophy and the "infinite fragility of her aspirations," Emma sees that she and people like her are not fragile.

> . . . The truth was that I could survive anything, that I was made of cast iron, and that I would spend my life not in protecting

105

myself but in protecting others from myself, starting with my children. . . .

Rosamund's prayer to God (in whom she does not believe, but feels is perhaps created by her need) is for Octavia's survival. She concludes, "If I didn't put me and mine first, they wouldn't survive." She finds strength in herself. She drives home with Octavia, who has recovered after the operation, past Queen's Crescent, significantly "ever demolished, ever renewed" and finds she can "take it and survive." Like Job, she has been threatened with the worst, and, like Job, she has kept her shape. She characteristically is convinced that any happiness she receives "hereafter" will be based on "fact and not on hope," an ineradicable rationalistic delusion, for what is a belief in survival but a hope? "Hereafter" too has unacknowledged overtones of heavenly rewards.

Clara does not like to admit the accidental, but acknowledges that chance has prevented her from being an eternal misfit. Her "moral inheritance of doubt" comes from her past, and she has both to escape her past and reconcile herself to it. She feels "absolved" by the institutional shape of her room, and in her confidences to Clelia finds a tone that "absolved her" and "redeemed her past."

She thinks of herself as a plant grown from seed sown in stony ground, who "grew by will and strain." A little later she decides she must have fallen where "a few grains of sand, a few drops of moisture" had supported her: "Because she would live, she would survive." Her faith in her own survival is shaken, temporarily, at her dying mother's bedside.

> It was possible, then, to go disastrously astray . . . survival was no certainty . . .

But later, she recovers her faith in herself and in life:

> Her mother was dying, but she herself would survive, even the guilt, because she had willed herself to survive, because she did not have it in her to die.

Clara's puritan will has been used on the side of life, of survival. Clara is appalled by the random scattering of human souls suggested by the parable of the sower. Rose, though, despite her morbidity, learns faith in the resilience and multiplicity of life. Even in her father's boring repetitions about the millions of people in the world, no two of them alike, she sees at last "true philosophic significance" and she makes an even greater discovery. Watching boys on the beach who catch crabs for fun and put them back again, she recognises at last "the true futility of joy."

When she is in the car with Simon, the pair of them note dead shrews, hedgehogs, a weasel. Simon can see only death, but Rose recognises that if nature is careless of the single life, it is careful of the type. She says,

> Yes, but there are so many dead because there are so many living . . . they're not really being killed off, it's where you don't see them on the roads that there aren't any in the hedges.

Simon misinterprets the true significance of the Manchester moth, the peppered moth that has evolved a black species to survive in the smoky industrial landscape, while the lighter ones have died off. He sees only "a grimy race of uniform lowliness" and concludes that progress and evolution are banal and adolescent preoccupations. But the Manchester moth in truth illustrates the marvellous resilience and adaptability of natural life.

Acknowledging the "green exhalations" which precede his own "rebirth" and "renewal," Simon

> touched, with his hand, the damp, raw pitted cells of the brick wall, themselves weathered into a semblance of organic life, and the smoky leaves of the ivy . . .

The ivy is fouled by industry, but industry's products can weather till they become part of the landscape. There can be some sort of mutual accommodation between nature and civilisation.

Emily, Rose's friend, quotes the poet: "Life is real, life is earnest, and the grave is not its goal, dust thou art to dust returneth was not spoken of the soul." But she cannot accept this comfort. She thinks of Malthus, and compares people with rats. Rose does not know whether Emily and Simon are right in agreeing that people should be shot.

> There was no knowing. I will leap off the ladder even blindfold into eternity, sink or swim, come heaven or hell. Like a rat, swimming through the dirty lake to the distant unknown shore.

Even in industrial landscapes, the human spirit survives: Rose has learned courage. She looks at one of the lions on Alexandra Palace, and finds it, though shoddy, preferable to the animals on the gates of her home: "elevated, aristocratic, hand-carved, unique with curled sneering lips and bared fangs." She prefers the

> shabby, mass-produced creature . . . it was gritty and cold, a beast of the people. Mass-produced, it had been, but it had weathered into identity. And this, she hoped, for every human soul.

All we can ask of life is to "weather into identity," in the face of violence, bloodshed, pollution and the inevitability of death. Rose says sadly of the civil war in Uhujudiana, "There isn't a peaceful nation on earth." She gets a begging letter from an anarchic magazine, and thinks that the writers of its manifesto seem to "see the world through the red blood of their own eyelids." In putting her faith in love and survival, Margaret Drabble does not deny the reality of evil. Emma sees a snake on her picnic with David and the children, after her reconciliation with David, with nature and with herself. There were snakes, even, Emma reflects, in the Garden of Eden.

> One just has to keep on pretending, for the sake of the children, not to notice.

One must find the courage to survive. Rose telling Simon of her troubles says, ". . . it would be funny, if I could think I'd survived it all." Simon replies, "You look as though you'd survived it." At another point, Rose says, "Cruel, isn't it, the way one keeps wanting things." But it is desire which keeps one alive, and attempts like those of Rose and Jane to suppress it by sacrifices to an imagined vengeful God are against the evolutionary current of life. Rose later realises that Christopher's desire to grab "herself, children, money, even parents-in-law" had proved "too strong for her will to renounce." Christopher is the healthy one. Rose recognises that with her background she grew up "incapable of relating: insecure, cold, undeveloped, guilt-ridden." She wonders "what freakish providence" has given her Christopher, so "obsessed with . . . possession that he refused to let her reject him?" She knows that Christopher, like Simon, has a "winning ticket": "they were real survivors" and so, to her surprise, she finds herself to be.

Even Jane, much possessed by death and the skull beneath the skin, lives on. She and James both pass through the valley of the shadow of death, but find resurrection. James believes his body will reassemble on the day of judgement. "Because bodies do, you know. They all come together again." Jane, who is afraid bodies will resolve into their elements, scatter like atoms or her lost collection of marbles, does not believe him. But after the accident, which they both feel is a "judgement" on them, James's body does come together again. He survives a double skull fracture, a broken arm and a broken pelvis.

Jane finds that in the crisis she is "shock-proof." Exposed to real disaster, she is shaken out of her enclosed world of imagined ones. At the time of the crash she has no thought for James: her instinct for survival asserts itself in her concern for the next generation: "All I cared for was the survival of my children."

She concludes later that James and Lucy are a "resilient couple." James "changed me forever and I am now what he made. I doubt, at times I panic, I lose faith: but doubt, as they say, is not accessible to unbelievers."

Like Yeats's Crazy Jane, Jane Gray learns to reconcile human love with God, death, decay and suffering. Talking to "The Bishop," Crazy Jane says, in accordance with Swedenborgian thought,

> For nothing can be sole or whole
> That has not been rent.

Jane Gray has been rent in childbirth and her mind has been rent in two, but she has survived, though her grip on life is less tenacious than that of the more robust characters.

Jane and James climb to the top of the Scar in the Pennines: "real, unlike James and me, it exists." James and she are, after all, on one level only characters in a book; on another this sense that their personalities and bodies are unreal is an expression of Jane's continuing mental disturbance. Such ambiguities enrich the book and help clarify its ultimate meaning: the difficulty of finding the truth.

The couple climb up to the top of the Scar,

where the grass has been worn away, into crumbling slippery earth, but we made it quite easily.

They climb a hill together, though the ground threatens to disintegrate beneath their feet, and share an experience of "the sublime." A "hilltop experience" is a slang phrase among theologians for such revelations. Like Emma, who has "become terrestrial . . . grown into the earth," Jane has found her footing at last. They find the tiny wild pansies called "Heart's ease."

Yet Jane, after the "sublime" experience on the hilltop, finds the whisky left overnight in the toothmug tastes "foul, ancient, musty, of dust and death" because she has spilled talcum powder into it. The pleasures of alcohol, like those of love, are tainted with intimations of mortality. "Let me wipe it first, it smells of mortality," says Lear before taking Gloucester's proffered hand in his own, in fellowship. James does not mind, sharing Jane's bed for the first time, that her hair is dirty and "smells of humanity." James and Jane, all lovers must, as chimney sweepers, come to dust, but love and fellowship are the only way of ameliorating the bleakness of life.

Love is incompatible with meanness, spiritual or financial, and meanness is not a trait Margaret Drabble can admire. The gifts of nature and of fortune, beauty, intellect and wealth are to be used and enjoyed, not thwarted and denied, as puritanism tries to do. In seeing riches as "a dreadful blight" and in regarding riches, beauty and brains as "mingled sources of pleasure and pain," Rosamund is denying the richness of life. So is Jane, in her terror of her poetic talent and her "true sexual beauty," which to her is a "menace and a guilt and a burden."

Spontaneous enjoyment should not be crushed or rooted out, as puritan asceticism taught, but cherished. When the body is bruised to pleasure soul, nature is frustrated in its purposes and potentialities. For Margaret Drabble, the true end of life is to reconcile flesh and spirit by accepting one's own nature and living with it, in a context of love and responsibility for others. While this is far from easy, and any accommodation achieved is costly, the reconciliation of instinct and morality remains as a possibility worth striving for. This reconciliation, the author hopes, can come about by involvement in society. In Ibsen's *Rosmersholm*, Rebecca West, who represents natural life and instinctive force against a puritanical culture, a civilised society, has to die in the millrace. Although the conflict is recognised by Margaret Drabble, her view of life is more flexible. The only character to die in her books is the indecisive Julian. She is concerned with the evolutionary power of survival. She concludes an article on Virginia Woolf in *Harpers Bazaar and Queen* (September 1972): "We owe it to her to survive." Her theology is tinged with pantheism, like that of Wordsworth, whom Emma comes to read with tears, and it is therefore on the outer edge of Christian orthodoxy. But her handling of religious ideas demonstrates depth and creative thought, especially in her own reworking of the concept of grace. Her reverence for nature, *Natura naturata*, is unforced, deep and sincere. Her acceptance of *natura naturans* costs her heroines (and so perhaps herself) more of a struggle. But her faith is in survival, through the powers of nature and through natural human love.

Puritanical withdrawal and isolation mean negation for Margaret Drabble. All her characters move, to greater or lesser degree, out of moralistic, self-centred isolation into involvement and love. In the first two books, as we have seen, this transition is uncertainly handled; in the third, *The Millstone*, Rosamund doesn't quite make it, but the treatment is successful and consistent in that we see the weight of conditioning Rosamund struggles against and only partially throws off. The conflict is fully and accurately worked out in terms of character and action. In *Jerusalem the Golden* there is a change of focus, but Clara too manages to get to the other side. There is some uncertainty of aim in the presentation of the Denham family, but it is through them and her (conventionally illicit) connexion with Gabriel that Clara learns to see, in all senses of the word, and to discover the possibility of love. The illicit affair in *The Waterfall* is Jane's salvation: for her the discovery of love brings with it a return to sanity. (Conventional sexual morality is defied by, and is irrelevant to, Jane, Clara and Louise, who must follow the dictates of their own hearts.) Rose's love for her children is constant, but to find healing she must move back to involvement with society through her husband. With this book Margaret

Drabble has travelled a long way from her first novel. In *A Summer Birdcage* we saw the difficulties of one egotistical young woman looking for social relationships: in *The Needle's Eye* we get a consideration of social relationships in contemporary industrial society. The book has its flaws, but it shows impressively Margaret Drabble's growth as a writer. (See Chapter 11.)

PART TWO

The Artist

8

The place of the arts

The transcendentality of God and corruption of everything pertaining to the flesh were antagonistic to sensuous culture of all kinds in religious life because of no use towards salvation . . . the Baptist denomination showed . . . an invincible antagonism to any sort of aristocratic way of life.—Max Weber.

Carlyle's father . . . considered "Poetry, Fiction in general . . . not only idle, but *false* and criminal."—W. E. Houghton.

Pushpin is as valuable as poetry.—Jeremy Bentham.

One can't have art without morality.—Jane, *The Waterfall.*

All art is quite useless.—Oscar Wilde.

> What cared Duke Ercole, that bid
> His mummers to the market place,
> What th'onion sellers thought or did?
> W. B. Yeats.

Many of Margaret Drabble's characters share the puritan suspicion of the arts. An artist herself, she has a very different view as expressed in her books.

Her most complete, though equivocal (see Chapter 10), statement about the arts comes in *Jerusalem the Golden.* There the arts, to which Clara makes her way not through her formal education but through contact with a family of rich artists, represent a whole way of life.

This culture takes centuries to grow, and embodies a set of values, a spiritual generosity, a richness older and more valuable than, completely antithetical to, the narrow penny-pinching utilitarianism in which Clara has been reared.

Clara, coming from the grim industrial north, finds in the Denhams (the father is a poet, the mother a novelist, Clara's friend Clelia a painter) the true culture that her grammar school and university have failed to give her.

Escape into their world (where Clara finds the radiant golden vision of her heavenly city) is Clara's version of salvation. She cannot trust her own eyes until liberated by the Denhams.

On a school trip to Paris,

> The Comédie Française seemed to her a collection of posturing gabbling shadows, mocking at plays she had studied in tranquillity and silence.

Clara can appreciate drama only on paper, not its living embodiment.

She is disappointed to find the celebrated mirrors of Versailles "all spotty." On her second visit, the mirrors in the hotel remind her of those others. This time she is with Gabriel, and her eyes have been opened. Now she sees the spots as "a source of pride and not of shame," the honourable marks of antiquity.

This time round, she sees, as she hopes to, a different Paris from the "architectural, linguistic fortress of her university days." In her schooldays she did not wish to "glimpse the exteriors of the houses of the famous dead. She wanted interiors." Now she has seen the interior of the Denham household, where she has her epiphany, her vision of the heavenly richness she has been seeking.

> The aristocratic ideal was vindicated. She stared at the golden eagle, so arrogantly and eternally poised, and wondered why she had ever thought birds on furniture were a bit off: why had she never bothered to look, why had she never asked herself what her eyes had told her? Why had she had to wait for such an education?

In this important passage, Clara sees the light of truth. The eagle, arrogant and aloof, "vindicates the aristocratic ideal" to which the Baptists were so opposed, and for which Clara has previously felt a "solid suburban scorn." Mrs Denham, like the room, is "poised equally between frayed charm and the austere splendour of riches." Clara has read her novel, *Custom and Ceremony.* The title comes from Yeats's poem, "A prayer for my daughter." "How but in custom and in ceremony," asks the poet, "Are innocence and beauty born?" Candida Denham and her books stand for the spiritual riches and freedom of inherited culture, values predating the industrial revolution which created Northam.

Faced in Gabriel's office with a picture of a pop singer, Clara is surprised to find pin-ups:

> she had thought that Gabriel's world would eschew, somehow, having no need of them, the cheaper glories of the masses.

Here Margaret Drabble pins down the grammar school girl like a butterfly. Clara agrees in surprise when Gabriel says the singer is beautiful. For a moment,

> she still did not see the point . . . collecting such things had always seemed to her from early school days on to be an indication of immaturity, of poverty, of lack of resources, of making do with second best: she had as resolutely and *puritanically* [my italics] scorned the pop world and its manifestations as her mother had done before her . . . she wondered what stubborn narrow prejudice had blinded her but an instant before.

The Denhams

> taught her, they instructed her, as once Miss Haines had taught her to admire Corneille: and the lesson about Corneille had been worthwhile, the object worthy of effort, so why not all these new acquisitions?

This sense of the value of effort, with an object in view, is part of Clara's puritan inheritance, reinforced by her formal education. But it failed to teach her the value of just looking, of believing what her eyes tell her.

Another shock for Clara is the Denham family photograph album, showing them with the famous.

> She had always been taught that such objects were . . . manifestations of the worst possible taste, as fatally revealing as a pet Alsatian dog on the window sill or ferrets in the back yard. . . . But the Denhams seemed unaware of the dreadful risk they were running.

In the full control of ironic wit here, the author makes us laugh, possibly out loud. But she is making a serious point. Looking at these pictures, Clara

> understood entirely, as she had never understood before, why one should wish to perpetuate such things, and why generation after generation had endeavoured to fix such moments into an eternity.

For love, surely was at the source of such conventional efforts: there had been love at every stage.

Through the commonplace image of the photograph album, two important values are celebrated: continuity, which makes culture like that of the Denhams possible, and love. Clara learns to appreciate continuity, though there is little of it in her own background to draw on. She can share the world of the Denhams, enjoy it, but her own nurture is so different she can never fully enter it. Her struggle has left her full only of "the will to love," but of love itself she is incapable.

But she finds other things she needs in this milieu. Listening at her first meeting with Clelia to a conversation which we are not given, she thinks Clelia's contribution

> implied a high intelligence, as well as a hopeful generosity of communication . . . she was in the presence of the kind of thing for which she had been searching for years . . .

Listening to Clelia, she knows she has at last found what she has been seeking for so long.

The Denhams, although the "golden nest" is too comfortable for their children to grow out of, although their garden runs to weeds, are to be valued highly: "Clelia was what she was." They represent quality: of mind, of spirit, of life. They are unselfconscious in their enjoyment of their fame and of their way of life. They show no puritanical strain, except for Gabriel, who has that unsatisfactory and inconsistent "strict inheritance."

The Denhams are unlike the couple in A *Summer Birdcage* who

> tended to believe that *objets d'art* ought to be kept in art galleries for the use of the public, so those they had collected were discreet, almost austere.

This couple exhibit a puritan guilt about individual possessions, though this does not inhibit them from being acquisitive. They collect, but in a shamefaced way which takes away the beholder's pleasure, by denying him any vision of artistic opulence, such as is offered by the Denhams.

The Denhams treasure the riches of the past. David Evans tells his wife Emma that like the modern wardrobe she objects to in their furnished house in Hereford he represents "modern life. In its less desirable aspects." As Emma is reconciled with

David at the end, we are presumably to take it that she becomes adjusted to "modern life." She has sided with Sophy Brent, "ripe" and "like a bowl of fruit," against the sterile correctness of her more conventional friend Mary, though again the link between modern life and nature seems dubious. We remember that David is an artist, an actor, like Sophy, but a better one. Emma enjoys the visual arts, particularly in their bright, shiny, speedy aspects.

So does Simon Camish's wife Julie, but Simon loathes "pop art, modern plays, television, owners of art galleries, interior decorators and modern furnishings with an almost undiscriminating passion." Simon has the preference for "sober utility to any artistic tendencies" attributed by Weber to the Quaker sect. Simon, explicitly puritanical, lives for his work. His wife's father

> like many self-made men . . . had an exaggerated respect for the powers of culture and education—he forced the children to attend concerts, plays . . .

Yet when Julie wants to go to art school, her father refuses to let her go around with "scruffy parasites." Here again is perceptive social observation. Simon is wrong, says the omniscient narrator, in assuming that Julie has no talent, and her frustration is doubtless due to this thwarting of her gifts. Simon, like Martin in *Jerusalem the Golden*, has no use for the decorative arts.

Neither has Rosamund. Her "visual sense" is "very weak." She shows the characteristics described by Lionel Trilling:

> . . . lack of imagination is a disease . . . which is endemic to the liberal mind. The liberal intellectual is always trying to establish principles, lay down rules, make distinctions in which to contain and order the welter of experience.

Rosamund is very much the "liberal intellectual" and we see her, throughout her book, trying to establish principles, lay down rules and make distinctions: she uses the word "anomaly" constantly. Rosamund rejects with boredom Joe's arts programmes on television. One is about drugs, and the other "even less interesting" is about the future of abstract art and the use of improvisation in the avant-garde Paris theatre. Escape into the drug scene, with its opportunities for hallucination and fantasy, would be contrary to Rosamund's analytical and positivist habits of mind. Abstract

119

art would certainly not interest her, and improvisation, drawing on sources of spontaneous creativity, outside the framework of rules laid down by a script, would seem to her a waste of time. As she admits herself, she is "wholly uncreative."

Rosamund has two novelist friends, Lydia and Joe. Joe writes successful books, which his friends agree to be bad. Lydia tries to do the same, but cannot finish her books. She envies Rosamund her education and her work, because it consists of sorting facts. But as we shall see, although Lydia has dried up after publishing only two novels, she can see truths not accessible to Rosamund.

Rosamund's conduct in an hotel where she spends a chaste night with her boyfriend is modelled on "cheap fiction" which they have both read a lot of. Young people read fiction to find out how grown-up life is lived, and when the scholarly Rosamund becomes pregnant she resorts to her gleanings from the same source. Rosamund is incapable of commitment and response to, real critical engagement with, serious fiction as against the cheap kind. She knows nineteenth-century novels are considered "worthier" than Elizabethan sonnet sequences, which she guiltily acknowledges to be a luxury subject.

The puritan, says Dr Erik Routley,

> is not happy about relaxing with fiction because fiction is "make-believe" and "make-believe" is, in any sense, anathema to a puritan.

Rosamund, reviewing a book on Defoe for an "unimportant magazine" is startled to find this attitude in herself and is upset about it.

> I have always maintained that I held an Aristotelian and not a Platonic view of fact and fiction.

(Aristotle held that poetry was "more philosophical" and more worthy of serious attention than history; Plato banished poets from his Republic on the grounds that their "lies" would teach bad morality and corrupt the state.) Yet despite the intellectual conviction given by her Cambridge training in literature, at heart Rosamund takes the puritan view. She is shocked to find that *Journal of the Plague Year* is fiction, not documentary. Her puritan sense of duty has driven her to read the whole of Defoe in order to write a review.

Because she is unaccustomed to coping imaginatively with fiction, she confuses Bunyan with his created character, Christian, in *Pilgrim's Progress.*

Octavia has chewed up Lydia's novel, based on events in Rosamund's life. Rosamund wonders what to say to Lydia, whether or not to pretend that Lydia had herself left the door open. Her puritan "honour," she feels, will make her confess her guilt.

Reading about herself in Lydia's novel, Rosamund is indignant at the way, "subtle enough technically", Lydia has hinted that

> the Rosamund character's obsession with scholarly detail and discovery was nothing more nor less than an escape route, an attempt to evade the personal crises of her life and the realities of life in general.

We recognise that the hint is true, and that Lydia, the creative writer, has seen and expressed a truth hidden from Rosamund, who prefers to collect and order facts. "Too much knowing is my vice" she thinks; but certain kinds of knowledge evade her. Despite her constant examination of her conscience, here is a truth about herself which she will not admit.

Lydia has had a miscarriage after being refused an abortion. Rosamund asks why Lydia doesn't put it in a book. Lydia says it would be unconvincing: that there is a difference between what happens in real life and what one can make real in art. "I don't like accidents in books," says Lydia.

> "So you don't think that because something happens, that makes it true?" I said. "No, not at all," said Lydia. "Do you?" "I suppose I must," I said.

In the puritan tradition, Rosamund prefers truth to fiction, which is why she has avoided nineteenth-century novels in order to collect data on Elizabethan poets, who raise fewer moral problems. A rationalist, she tends to class "scarlet letter" literature as the "fantasies of repressed imagination."

When Octavia is in hospital for a heart operation, Rosamund thinks of Ben Jonson, who said, "my sin was too much hope of thee, loved boy." After years of professional concern, at a high academic level, with poetry, she can still say

> we too easily take what the poets write as figures of speech, as pretty images or strings of bons mots.

121

This failure to grasp the essential seriousness of poetry is a limiting judgement on Rosamund, who has indeed been using her studies as an evasive game. Now, suffering and fearing for Octavia, she makes the discovery about poets which amazes her: "Sometimes they speak the truth." Her previous failure to recognise the validity, the truth, of poetry comes from her puritanical preoccupation with classifiable fact.

As we have seen from her social relationships (in which she is always polite, correct and reserved, but remote and ungiving), the imaginative sympathy which literature, poetry as much as fiction, demands is beyond her. She finds a "certain poetic justice" in Lydia's misfortune. Lydia had "exposed" Rosamund and Octavia in her book, and Octavia has punished Lydia by chewing it up. Rosamund, whose withdrawn hardness we have already noted, is "curiously satisfied at some level" at Lydia's dismay, "that she actually blenched." Rosamund's limitations are here beautifully dramatised and displayed: she enjoys her petty revenge, she has no pity for poor Lydia whose creation has been destroyed, and of which there is no carbon copy, and she fails to recognise that penetration beneath the surface, that vision of truth, which is the novelist's function and achievement. Yet Rosamund is a teacher of English literature. In the depiction of her characteristic limitations, there is real solidity and subtlety.

Even Simon, who hates most forms of art, can do better than Rosamund. His mother is a writer who specialises in cheery, cosy accounts of her hardships. At Oxford he is embarrassed about her, as she is a "joke name" like Patience Strong or Godfrey Winn. He feels when young that she falsifies her grim experience, but later realises that it is the fact of expression that counts: it is a "true transcendence of hardship."

Clara, who has studied Corneille with pleasure, does not realise that tragedy is possible in real life till she comes face to face with evidence of her dying mother's former aspirations.

Jane the poet thinks "I lie to you because I lie with you"

> the loveliest of ambiguities, though sadly restricted to one language; untranslatable, and therefore lacking the absolute truth that seemed to inform it.

122

As a poet she relishes ambiguity, and recognises the limits of communication across different languages. Only a truth which can be expressed in all tongues can be "absolute" and universal for her. Jane is of course looking for absolutes and universals in the welter of her experience. The unspoken question is whether any truth can be expressed in all languages, by all kinds of people with different habits, from different cultures? Ultimately the only general truth Jane can arrive at is that truth is itself limited and subjective.

Hers is a novel partly about the difficulties of writing a novel. At times Jane alienates us, in the Brechtian sense, by pointing out that the novelist, the creator, may choose any conclusion he or she pleases. Her lover might have been killed in the accident, which would have been a fine "poetic justice"; he might have been maimed, or made impotent ("a little, twentieth-century death"). But, Jane writes, "there is no conclusion." She refuses to give us the neat solutions offered us by art, but denied us by life, which continues on its way without end, like the waterfall of the title. *The Waterfall* is a complete and satisfactory statement about the relations between art and life, and the nearest to being a flawless work of art in itself that Margaret Drabble has produced.

Jane writes:

> I have lied, but only by omission. Of the truth, I haven't told enough. I flinched at the conclusion, and can even see in my hesitance a virtue: it is dishonest, it is inartistic, but it is a virtue, such discretion, in the moral world of love.

She feels description is "treachery" and compares herself to Africans who defend their loved ones from photography. In the Freudian terms in which she often thinks, Jane is here reverting to a "primitive" belief, which causes her artistic trouble. How can a novelist write without describing? It is not true, either, that her lies are only lies of omission. Her self-contradictions reveal the truth to us.

When Malcolm tries for a reconciliation at the time Jane is about to go on holiday with James, she admits that her earlier accusation of homosexuality against Malcolm was not the truth. Her violence to him on the telephone

> had been motivated wholly by my need to preserve my future— my non-existent, brief future—with James, but in part at least by

123

real sexual jealousy . . . Malcolm had managed to escape me to live with another woman, and a musical woman at that. . . .

Similarly, she claims to have become completely frigid after Laurie's birth. But if her body had been as completely "closed" to Malcolm as she claims, how did he manage to give her Bianca?

Her conviction of frigidity is apparently as exaggerated as her guilt. She is convinced that she has murdered Malcolm, who was singing a song by Campion about love and murder when she met him.

> I murdered him in the true lyrical sense, by rejection, by the lending and withdrawal of my beauty . . . murder isn't lovely as it is in that poem, it is hideously ugly, unspeakably shamefully ugly, in vain do the poets try to disguise and excuse and purify these things, in vain do they try to dignify their own rejection by dignifying cruelty and scorn. They suffered, they bled.

Jane shows an attitude to fiction similar to Rosamund's. Rosamund evaded the moral challenges posed by fiction by choosing to research into Elizabethan sonnets. But Jane finds moral difficulties even in a song of love (which in characteristic Elizabethan fashion links love with death).

> I blame Campion, I blame the poets, I blame Shakespeare for that farcical moment in *Romeo and Juliet* where he sees her at the dance, from afar off, and says, I'll have her, because she is the one that will kill me.

Jane is angry with the poets for delivering, in Sir Philip Sidney's words, a "golden" world, when reality is so cruel. She implies, like Plato, that art is immoral because it lies. We never see any of Jane's own poems, though we are told they get into print.

She acknowledges even her poetic gift with guilt. She does not like the notion of "unique blessings, unique gifts," yet writes of her conviction that she is "uniquely gifted." Worried about inequality, she morbidly denies her own nature and this is partly responsible for her breakdown. She is ashamed to admit to James at the start of their affair that she still writes poetry, but later confesses it to the reader.

In her misery,

> The only thing left to me to want to do was poetry: I wrote constantly, badly, with passion, and with flashes of alarming satis-

faction, flashes that seemed to shine back at me, reflected from another brighter source of light.

Her art is here a dual symbol: the "light" with its overtones of salvation is what she is seeking; and her attitude to her art is symbolist, in which art reflects the transcendent reality of other, greater worlds.

Writing is also a cure for her grief.

> The more unhappy I was the more I wrote: grief and words were to me inseparably connected, and I could see myself living out that maxim of literary criticism which claims that rhyme and metre are merely ways of regularising and making tolerable despair.

She thinks she tries hard to impose order upon her work because she is "unnaturally aware" of her "helpless subjugation" to her gift. But again she is dramatising herself and casting herself in a passive role. She tries to create order in her art because her life is so chaotic. To wrestle with the problems of real life, her own sickness (in order to heal which, according to D. H. Lawrence, the novelist writes), she turns to the novel form. She has lost her poetic gift, after finding James:

> I did not know how to write about joy, I could find no words for the damp and intimate secrets of love.

In Zola she finds the opposite tendency to the prettification which to her seems so culpable in the Elizabethan poets: he likes to turn his characters into corpses, she thinks. "In his life," wonders Jane, "perhaps he was more charitable to the flesh?" Here again she is using literature in her characteristic fashion, interpreting it in the light of her own need. She seeks charity towards her own flesh.

She thinks

> writing is a thing one can do anywhere, in a hotel bedroom, in solitary confinement, in a prison cell, a defence more final, less destructible than the company of love.

Perhaps we see here Jane's real problem: has she partly chosen her isolation, in order to be able to write? There is an inscription in Paris, mentioned in *Jerusalem the Golden*, that "the artist's well loved pain strengthens him." Jane reflects that some of her poems are "none the worse for the fact that they were founded on an unfulfilled terror." Jane has possibly sought pain to feed her imagination, or at least in finding it has made a virtue of necessity. Her success in finding suffering in two different sexual relationships may convict her of this form of masochism.

When her gift has temporarily left her, during her brief and partial happiness with James, she tells him

> rhymes in verse are a trivial matter, as trivial as playing cards, as pointless as fast cars. . . .

Yet she finds herself able to write again when James lies shattered in the hospital, coming slowly back to life.

But although a poet herself (and Margaret Drabble convinces us by creating thought-processes appropriate to a poet that she is one), Jane shares the puritan anxiety about the validity of the arts. "One can't have art without morality," she insists. Not for her Oscar Wilde's apparently frivolous, but profound, formulation that "all art is quite useless." The puritan conscience demands that art should serve a moral purpose. Jane for this reason chooses to reject James's skills, in their lesser fashion also arts, of card tricks and lovemaking. She agrees that his talent is "perverse: a sinister dexterity." Sinister means literally left-handed, but also carries the meaning of dangerous and immoral. At bottom, she has the same distrust for her own gifts as a writer, because of her morbid conscience.

Her husband Malcolm is a true artist, with integrity. A guitarist and singer,

> he does not descend towards the popular; he is a purist, a musician, and just good enough to be able to afford to be so, even in so competitive a world.

Jane has no interest in music: there are no musical experiences in Margaret Drabble's books. Her heroines unpack their hearts with words. But Malcolm's singing appeals to Jane characteristically because of its "impersonal purity": his voice has a "choirboy's innocent assertion," and she is looking for innocence.

Jane's attitude to the arts, like Rosamund's, is skilfully integrated into plot and characterisation, and both subtly exemplify the puritanism of the characters.

The artistic and human responsibilities of the novelist are considered in Margaret Drabble's first novel, *A Summer Birdcage.* Stephen, Louise's husband, is inadequate both as a novelist and as a man. A sadistic and neglectful husband, he lives on the profits of his father's tobacco factory and indulges in doublethink about lung cancer. His novels are satirical, snobbish and bitchy.

They lack compassion, but Sarah's greatest objection is that they deal only in externals:

> they don't seem to add up to anything. They don't imply the truth.

Sarah goes on:

> Satire won't do. Worldliness won't do. But until you can do them both you can't do anything. Immaturity is no good, and they made me feel immature, all those people . . . the thing is I couldn't start to feel them in my terms because I couldn't really feel them in theirs, and one needs a double background. Perhaps it can be learned by a long apprenticeship and dedicated exploration. Perhaps nobody is born with it. Perhaps it is only me that takes refuge in things like chance . . . cars in the night . . .

The first quotation is about art: the second is about both novel-writing and the art of living, of creating a common human bond in order to understand, so that artistic creation can present the truth. In this book the necessity is recognised, although the ideal is neither fully achieved nor satisfactorily dramatised.

Louise's lover, John, is a professional actor, a former "king of the ADC" (Cambridge's amateur dramatic club, cradle of much professional talent).

Sarah is ambivalent about the theatre world, and satirical about its enclosed self-absorption.* She feels too that actors seem to be

> so obvious, as though looking like an actor were half the job of being one. Perhaps it is. A devotion to forms and ceremonies

* A real-life example of this occurred when I went to the Arts Theatre wardrobe in Cambridge for costumes when I was helping produce a school play. I admired a tiny-waisted costume. The wardrobe mistress told me it was used in *A Midsummer Night's Dream.* "The girl's name was Margaret . . . Margaret . . . I can't remember her other name, but she used to play leads at the ADC and she married Clive Swift." This was in 1967, when Margaret Drabble was on the way to becoming a household name.

and darlings and anecdotes: what artist or poet would ever say they loved art galleries or literary cocktail parties in the infatuated way in which actors say they love the theatre?

As we have seen, Sarah has a puritan conscience, and "forms and ceremonies" are alien to the puritan mentality, something to be treated with suspicion. But despite her intellectual disapproval, the theatre world has its attractions for her. An overdressed actress at a party

> looked ghastly, but I preferred her ghastliness to everything else I felt around me.

This is because the woman is striking and dramatic, "among all those other subtle women in that subtle Greek decor." Sarah enjoys being in John's dressing-room, which is "messy and very human," so different from "Stephen's meaningless Greek womb."

> I began to see why Louise fled there so often for refuge . . . whatever it lacked, it had life in excess, dirty, exaggerated life.

Sarah associates the theatre and its "life" with freedom: she is a wanderer herself and has always preferred "vagrants to inhabitants." She thinks, naively, that she would like to try acting as a career: "If I could. It must be fun, letting rip in public like that."

Both Sarah and Emma consider actors to be "megalomaniacs," but both recognise the vitality, however grudgingly they do so, beneath the passion for self-display. Sarah considers John's "megalomania" to be due to "real excess of energy and not . . . sheer blinkered ambition."

> Once he said to a director who told him not to overact: "How can you overact life?"

Emma finds in the theatre only "fake smells of dust and varnish and sawdust and size" but Emma resents her husband's career for ruining her own and has consequent malice towards it. For her the theatre is "one huge irrational sham, made for fantasy and fiction, not for fact." Emma has retreated from metaphysical speculation into the collection of factual information; she has the puritan distrust of make-believe and like Rosamund has little use for the imagination (at least until Emma discovers the truth of Wordsworth, as Rosamund discovers the truth of Ben Jonson).

Emma is not even interested in facts about the theatre: "David at least knew better than to talk to me of cycloramas and revolves." She finds drama and the theatre unreal because

> real conflict for me . . . always turns out to be wordless . . . we conflict because we cannot communicate, because there is nothing to be said. I know realism is not all, but to me it is all, and anything that does not seem to be dredged up from a fleshly occurrence leaves me undisturbed. Symbols and images, oh yes, I have heard of them.

But they mean nothing to her. Her husband says he acts to "discover about" himself: "with each new part I play, I find out more about me." Emma finds

> something touching and pathetic in David's assertion of his own positive wonderful self: poor David, who has no more self than a given quantity of water, and who is always trying to contain his own flowing jelly-like shapelessness in some stern mould or confine, because he is I think afraid of the aimlessness of his own undirected violence.

It is difficult to know whether this judgement of Emma's on her husband is objective and sound, or distorted by malice. It may even be a projection of her own struggle to define herself. But David uses his art for self-discovery, to find a mould, and the search is surely one of the things life is all about. Emma says of an unpleasant American journalist:

> He had nothing of that superficial goodwill and interest and keenness and apparent love that is so widespread amongst actors that I sometimes think it must not be superficial but profound.

As in the Denham household, the arts are associated with the primary value of human love. They are "on the side of life." Emma recognises the communal bond among the acting fraternity and associates herself with its world. Sophy Brent represents the "life, exaggerated life" that Sarah in the previous book found in John's dressing-room. Emma and Rosamund, in learning about life, come to appreciate and value poetry. This recognition is part of, and a product of, their greater maturity.

The arts cement community, celebrate love and continuity, and by telling the truth open the beholder's eyes to the richness of life. Despite her feeling that the Denham world must, somehow, despite the plants and swimming fishes there, carry within it the seeds of decay, Margaret Drabble hopes with Matthew Arnold, in his preface to *Culture and Anarchy*, that

> . . . culture . . . leads us . . . to conceive of the true human perfection as a *harmonious* perfection, developing all sides of our humanity.

Arnold accuses the "Nonconformists, the successors and representatives of the puritans" of having

> developed one side of their humanity at the expense of all the others and have becoming incomplete and mutilated men in consequence. Thus, falling short of harmonious perfection, they fail to follow the true way of salvation.

All Margaret Drabble's leading characters are "incomplete and mutilated" in some way, all deformed by guilt and the puritan conscience. Many of her minor characters are artists (only Jane combines the roles of artist and intellectual, among leading characters) and her work shows continuing and intelligent reflection on the place of the arts in society. This preoccupation is integrated both with her social panorama and her persistent analysis of the puritan inheritance and the possibilities of salvation. "Culture" for her means not the formal educational process, but the liberalising and humanising effect of the arts. They are a means towards salvation, for they help the individual to grow and to understand love.

9

Images, duplicity

> All thought becomes an image and the soul
> Becomes a body. . . .
>
> W. B. Yeats

Like other serious novelists, Margaret Drabble uses tangible objects
and settings suggestively, with symbolic value. Some of her
symbols are explicit, created only to serve expressive functions.
At other times she exploits the ambiguities lying in everyday
turns of phrase. Her novels show a progression from intellectual
analysis to a growing power in handling symbolic detail to create
multi-layered textures.

A key word in her books is "duplicity." Clara searches among
the improving literature of her childhood for the

> true brittle glitter of duplicity, for the warm shine of wider, more
> embracing landscapes; she looked for half-truth, for precious
> qualification, for choice, for possible rejections . . .

Emma finds in the silly conversation of Sophy Brent the
promises of a "rare verbal duplicity," which is puzzling until
one has read the later book and realises that Emma is looking
for the same richness of experience as Clara.

Jane speaks of her "duplicity" in leaving her son behind, cry-
ing, at his nursery school, when she has promised to come back.
On one level, she means she is deceiving the child, but the word
"duplicity" has wider meanings within the story's context. Jane
is also deceiving her cousin Lucy by sleeping with Lucy's husband, and is herself a split personality. Jane is a poet and exploits the ambiguities latent in the words she uses. So, with
increasing confidence and skill, does her creator.

Tumbledown houses in Margaret Drabble's books mean houses divided against themselves, barely able to stand, paralleling the bad repair of the inhabitants' relationships.

An exception to the generalisation that people whose marriages seem to be crumbling live in crumbling houses is Simon, but even here there is consistency, as his house (like his marriage) is held together by his wife's money.

The Denham house, an aristocratic mansion full of old and beautiful things, has a "lonely eminence . . . an air of somewhat tragic survival" among miscellaneous later buildings.

Public buildings, too, are used significantly. In Northam, the bookshop which Clara treats unofficially as a free library is "a charming building that dated, almost alone in the town, from the pre-industrial epoch." The values it enshrines are pre-industrial, too, the literary culture that Clara aspires to.

The new public library in *The Needle's Eye*, however, is

> A modern building of spectacular ugliness, a low inadequate building disgraced by its surroundings as it disgraced them. In the spring, sometimes, it looked all right. . . .

The pub where the bad Eileen hangs out with her Hell's Angels is modern.

> It had a forecourt where stone mushrooms served as seats, and plants grew out of pots from a topsoil of fag ends.

Both public library and public house are ugly because they both deny the organic. The library can be softened by spring flowers, but the pub is an even worse perversion. Instead of real, edible mushrooms there are stone ones, and plants grow not in nourishing soil but out of the burnt-out, cancer-inducing waste and rubbish of industrial society.

Clara's school is on a "muddy waste of grass and tarmac." A bomb

> had fallen during the war, on a neighbouring chapel, and the site had been levelled out and was now an unofficial part of the school's playgrounds.

For Clara the road to salvation is not through religion. The house of God has been blasted out of existence. Its functions, its promises and its premises have been taken over by modern secularised education, as Ivan Illich has pointed out. Training as a teacher, Clara takes a course in "non-denominational religion."

In *The Waterfall,* the Blackwall tunnel, with its tiled white walls, its "deadly pallid fluorescent glare" is compared by James to fairyland, because of its pretty lights. Jane with James and her children is physically in a mundane tunnel, lit by artificial light. Jane and James laugh, but Jane does not deny what he says. For her James has transformed the tunnel into a magic playground; her need has changed the commonplace reality of a route which offers a substitute for an open-air road. This transformation is characteristic, as Jane is agoraphobic and prefers enclosed spaces, and describes her state as "having split myself . . . gone underground." The transformation in her mind is perhaps even justified by the contrast between the name "Blackwall" and the white, bright reality. Eventually James brings them out of the tunnel, "into the open air," just as he rescues Jane from her enclosed, withdrawn state.

Furnishings, too, can be significant. Simon comes from a home which has been polished with loving care, despite threadbare carpets, coconut matting, badly laid lino and utility furniture:

> a life too near the bones of subsistence, too little padded, too severely worn.

Polish "had been a veneer, a thin and penetrable barrier against scorn and decay."

> Cleanliness costs you nothing, his mother used to say: a statement not wholly accurate, as she must have observed herself when adding up her grocery bills.

The subject matter of the book, as we shall see, is money. Professor Harrison writes:

> Standards of housewifery were high, with much emphasis on scrubbing and scouring and polishing. . . . Nowhere did the great Victorian virtues of frugality, cleanliness and sobriety appear . . . to greater purpose than in the cottage homes of England.

Simon comes from a cottage home, where frugality, cleanliness and sobriety have been practised, and which have left indelible marks on his own character. The loving care with which the polish has been applied has, too, overtones of the "social polish" to which Mrs Camish aspires, in herself and for her son.

Visiting Nick and Diana's, Simon notes that there is no polish in their house: chairs are painted, metal and marble predominate. The glasses are "thick and heavy, with no sparing of substance." Being rich, Nick and Diana can afford solidity of texture, without top dressing.

Nick works in television. Television for Margaret Drabble represents a milieu in which people have opportunities for self-display. Marshall McLuhan once said in a television interview, "TV is an X-ray medium," but Margaret Drabble recognises that it deals, in fact, with reflections of surfaces. For Simon, the television world is

> a garden of idleness . . . where bright young middle aged people stood about on burgeoning, sprouting carpets and drank large drinks and watched their own reflections, discreetly, in mirrors and eyes.

Watching one's own reflection is a neat image for the conditions of television work, as performers watch themselves on monitor screens and on video tape. The image also embraces this dinner party, where television performers are indulging in self-centred exhibitionism.

Women are mentioned as wearing peacock feathers, symbols of self-regarding vanity. Conversation turns to "the new boardroom dramas on ITV." In this novel about industrial society, the world of appearances represented by this party of television people and the world of commerce which is the main theme of the book are fused in one realistic, seemingly trivial, image.

Eating and drinking also have significance. Emma prefers to eat *hors d'oeuvres*, and generally prefers preliminaries to adult experience. When Clara thinks she has lost Gabriel, she sits over a cup of coffee.

> She did not know what she wanted: she bowed her head, sadly, saddened, staring into her small bitter black cup, seeing there the bitter limits of her own hitherto illimitable designs.

The bitter cup is a familiar image of an inescapable, grim reality. Clara's gesture is also significant. Her bowed head indicates acceptance, submission to circumstance. In a small kitchen, a secret kiss, in a "dangerous angle, backs to the wall," excites her as the very height of passion. Clara fights for the life she wants: her back is always to the wall.

Clara meets Gabriel for lunch in the Oriental department of Liberty's. She loses her way there, in the world into which she is being liberated, and she is also taking "liberties" with Gabriel's marriage. She loses her way because the exotic environment of foreign artefacts is strange to her. When she finds Gabriel and they have lunch together, she admires a trellis pattern of cream on her soup. She has realised that the arts are dependent upon slow-growing tradition, and says, "I could never make it in a hundred years." Gabriel says ". . . it's started to spread already. Much better to do it yourself, than to let it go."

And she put her spoon in, and stirred and drank.

Two pages later, Clara is lying with Gabriel on his office floor. The act of drinking represents Clara's decision about experience. Her rapacity is destructive. Playing with Clelia's Japanese wooden egg puzzle, she "disorganises" it. Clelia fails to reassemble it: like Humpty Dumpty, the egg cannot be put together again. Clara's first sexual experience with Gabriel takes place in his office, the setting which gives him his significance for her. The television world is "instinct with glamour" for Clara. Although she is not a virgin and Gabriel is married, their coming together is a sort of bridal. The small round paper punchings from his secretary's machine fill Clara's hair like confetti as they lie there. The confetti, like Clara's loving, is a shoddy, commercial-industrial makeshift.

One of industry's most characteristic and widespread products is the car. None of Margaret Drabble's emancipated women seems to have acquired a driving licence. Cars are driven by sexy, dangerous men, whirling women on journeys into illicit passion. Set on collision courses, these cars bring their own punishment in the form of crashes.

This ambivalence about cars betrays Margaret Drabble's own anxieties about submitting to "spontaneous enjoyment" which, according to Weber, the puritan tries to destroy, although her books show that intellectually she would like to endorse it. Emma admits that Wyndham has been little more to her than "a dangerous high-powered object, like his own fast car." When he crushes her legs by accident against the garage door, she feels she has been justly punished.

Jane also feels herself punished for adultery by an accident in her lover's car, but the car symbol is here used in a more subtle, ambivalent and artistic way, weaving through the book into a meaningful pattern. James is part-owner of a garage and drives a Maserati at a "horrible speed." For Jane, preoccupied with death, car bodies are "rusty corpses." Racing cars frighten her, as a menace of death. The decision taken by James and a colleague to drive round a race-track reminds Jane of

> some unmentionable conspiracy, like the subversive conspiracy of sex.

There is a "curious dangerous sulphurous burning smell" from the track, implicitly the smell of hell and damnation, which Jane associates both with cars and with sex.

Nevertheless, Jane enjoys the "deafening irregularly rhythmic roar" of motorcyclists. Her attitude to passion, as we have seen, is profoundly ambivalent.

As they roll along the dual carriageway on their way to an illicit holiday in Norway, the radio starts to play a pop song (originally a much anthologised poem) called "Chimborazo, Cotopaxi," an escape song, as Jane observes, about remote, faraway and desirable places. Like their holiday, the song is cut off before it can really start. Jane is wearing her safety-belt when the crash occurs. Even unbuckled, it prevents her from being thrown out. Characteristically, James is not wearing his safety-belt and suffers near-fatal injuries.

For a while after the accident, Jane despises James's interest in cars.

> He had talked of response, as the car took off along the road, as her body flung itself from him, but what idiocy to equate a machine and a woman, neurotics though both of them were: a lump of expensive metal, a mechanical toy, and she herself not so much better, like a machine.

In her revulsion after the accident, which brings what she sees as enlightenment, but later rejects, Jane recognises that it is idiocy to equate a machine and a woman but then proceeds to do just that. She is reverting to her schizoid view of the world. One of the definitions of schizophrenic madness is the inability to distinguish one's own body from inanimate surrounding objects.

In classing both cars and women as "neurotics," Jane is manifesting the symptoms which at other times she denies having truly suffered.

She achieves some sort of healing when her son sees a put-it-together-yourself kit for a Formula One Ferrari. He wants it because it looks like his Uncle James's. Jane struggles to put it together for him. She "has never been good with" her hands.

> The words in the assembly instructions meant nothing to me at all, despite their familiarity: how could I identify such things as rear axles, large gear wheels, hub caps and exhaust stacks?

She spends hours poring over the diagram, trying to fit the right bits into the right places. In the end she manages to stick it together, but it will not move, although it "whirrs into life." Finally, she pushes two bits of the assembly together and the thing starts to move, "like a beetle," across the carpet.

When faced with a real life practical task, Jane finds that words, the materials she uses to create her poetry, are inadequate. In putting together a box of fragmented pieces into something capable of moving, in a semblance of organic life, she is on the way to putting herself together again. By pushing two separated pieces together, she is symbolically healing the split in her own psyche. Significantly, this effort is made on behalf of her child. She has, after the disaster in which she risked his security and his life, awakened once more to her responsibility for him.

Eventually, Jane is glad that James did not give up driving after the accident. Lucy, his wife, has lost interest in racing cars and speaks of the race-tracks with that "mixture of envy and contempt with which clever women talk about beautiful women and expensive clothes"—with hostile suspicion of spontaneous enjoyment. Jane learns to like fast driving:

> I liked ripping along fast roads with him . . . pretending I was some other kind of person entirely. I liked to pretend he was mine.

Jane has accepted passion in her life, although aware of its dangers and the possibilities of corruption. She has succumbed to spontaneous enjoyment, sinful though it still seems to her, and though she knows she must pay for it in suffering. In this acceptance she finds something like a restoration of health and expresses most satisfactorily the truth about the relationship between puritanism and permissiveness.

Jane is a poet, and words and images in *The Waterfall* are used with a wonderful resonance and ambiguity. Their meanings shift from context to context as she contradicts herself. The "waterfall" of the title is a card trick in which James dovetails two halves of a pack of cards into one, an image of their sexual union. But Jane also has doubts about the validity of their relationship, and may have built her hopes on a house of cards. A recurrent image in Margaret Drabble's work, particularly in this book, is the current of life, and this is a novel about the relations between art and life. An (unfortunately untraceable) writer has said, in haunting phrase, that physical life has the continuity and consistency "of a flame or of a waterfall." What appears permanent is in fact a flux, in a constant state of change and motion.

Jane lives in fear of dissolution: she has no confidence in life. But her experience belies her fears. She and James both survive, although both are changed by their experiences. Alienated from life, Jane plays alienation games in the Brechtian sense, by telling us that she could supply alternative endings if she liked. But she lets James stay alive, because (she says) he did in fact do so. This confusion is resolved when we grasp that Jane is writing an autobiographical novel about "real" experiences, which she fails to distance fully. She can find no order in her experience, considers she has failed in her task.

Jane's vision is confused by her neurosis. She is over-concerned with blood. The word "blood" is used in its literal sense at least eighteen times; the verb "bleed" occurs twice; there is mention of a "bleeding" womb and after a tree is uprooted it leaves red "bleeding" earth. Although Jane may have Mark Antony's speech ("thou bleeding piece of earth") in *Julius Caesar* in mind, attributing to earth the capacity to bleed seems more likely to be just another schizophrenic image. "Bloody" is used in its literal sense several times, and once in its slang sense. Lucy complains of poverty and says to Jane that Jane's husband must be making "a bloody fortune." The phrase implies success at the expense of others, the thing Jane is most afraid of, and suggests that there is no money to be made without guilt. When Jane writes poetry,

the ink was pouring on to the sheets like blood. My sublime blood, my sublimated blood.

Writing means for Jane, as it meant for Milton, the "precious lifeblood of a master spirit": she is afraid she is uniquely gifted. The ink like blood on the sheets of paper recalls the blood of childbirth which had stained the cloth sheets of her marriage bed, in which she first sleeps with James, a few days after her baby is born. The blood on the sheets is also an indication that her true virginity was given to James, confirmed in that she had held on to her virginity "in wise alarm, through marriage, through childbirth," because she is afraid that knowledge, true carnal knowledge of another person, will destroy her. Her mind draws "blood and sustenance" from its own guilt and she ponders continually on blood in the sense of kinship, the "Freudian family nexus": "Blood is blood," she muses.

Blood pours from James's head after the accident, and Lucy tells her that after a previous car crash the "rust-coloured water had been seeping on to the road."

It is the fluidity of blood that frightens Jane: "so liquid we are inside our stiff bodies, so easily resolving into other elements." She is afraid that James will die: "be beautifully resolved into his constituent elements." Her house is damp, she sweats a lot and is terrified of the wetness of making love. Ultimately a blood clot, the result of the contraceptive pill, is the price she must pay for love.

Images of blood are linked with those of cards and gambling (and Jane is preoccupied with winning and losing) in:

perhaps after all I only allowed myself to lose so badly because I knew that I held in my concealed hand a trump card, and that at the end of the game I would fling it down, the ace of hearts, gaping red, and that James would fall into my arms and die there?

Believing she is uniquely gifted, she sees her own heart as an ace. Like Margaret Drabble's other clever women, she puts a high value on her gifts, though her arrogance is mixed with diffidence. Jane hopes to win by sacrificing her own heart. It gapes red, it is the source of her lifeblood. To offer one's heart in love is to tear it, metaphorically, from one's own bosom.

> "I'll pawn you this heart from my bosom,
> Only say that you'll love me again,"

says the Carter family song. The words Jane uses, "gaping red," suggest wounds and suffering, as well as auricles, ventricles, veins and arteries. If she were to "fling down" her bleeding heart, James could die in her arms. Even then there is another ambiguity: in Elizabethan poetry—and Jane is a well-read poet, with a degree in English—to "die" is used punningly in the sense of to have an orgasm. Morbidly, Jane cannot rid herself of the association between sexual pleasure and death. "Jane Grey/ Head on the block" she muses, and sees the appropriateness of her own name to her role as sacrificial victim.

But as well as victim she sees herself as "murderess." She is convinced that she has "murdered" her husband Malcolm.

> When the murderess chooses the role of victim, when she arrays herself in shabby clothes, slopping down to the shop on the corner in her slippers and her apron, what disasters is she inviting, what massacres, what inverted cruelty, what blood will she not see flow?

The mention of the "shop on the corner" roots her agony in everyday reality for us. It is also an image of the communal life Jane has withdrawn from: she lacks the courage to ask the grocer for a pound of sprouts. She has sunk into solitude, as though it were her "natural element." Withdrawing because she is afraid of her own passions, she feels herself insubstantial, but capable of shattering others into fragments.

Meeting James for the first time with her family, she feels that if he were to rise violently to his feet, the whole room would collapse like paper: that if he were to speak,

> decades of careful pretence would shatter at the sound of his own voice like old dead flesh exposed to alien air.

When she is in her parents' home, she is afraid that any movement, her mere existence, "might shatter them all into fragments." James's business dealings are for her "thin papery structures."

Lacking faith in life, Jane sees insubstantiality, fragmentation, dissolution everywhere. Her own identity is fluid and dissolved. As a child, she collected marbles. She still has the box in which she kept them, though the marbles are all lost, "though, presumably, like atoms still intact." In the slang phrase, Jane has "lost her marbles," that is her sanity. Furthermore, they are scattered "like atoms," the constituent elements she is afraid she and James will disintegrate into. But she still has the box the marbles used to be kept in. She is still within her own body, still alive, although her mind is split into at least two pieces. When she had her marbles, her full powers of intellect, they represented impossibly bright hopes. But with experience and disappointment they have dispersed. It is also in keeping with her obsessive character to hoard and collect with no specific purpose, and as an artist she appreciates the beauty of those whorled pieces of glass. In inventing a narrator-poet, Margaret Drabble draws on the resources of language, of metaphor and suggestion, richly and creatively.

The images of blood recall *Macbeth*, another story of destructive guilt. Jane quotes the play at one point: "What, in our house, as Lady Macbeth said when true emotion failed her." Jane is afraid at times that her emotions are not real, that nothing about her is real. When Malcolm gives Jane a black eye, she tries to wash off the bruise, which she sees as a sign of her guilt, having driven him to it. We are reminded of Lady Macbeth's attempts to wash her hands.

After the birth of Bianca, when Jane has slept chastely with James,

> "I'll wait for you," she said: long dead through all her bandages, ripped and defeated, she committed herself to waiting.

The "bandages" soak up the blood of childbirth, but also give us an image of Lazarus, usually pictured as bandaged, who was brought back from the dead. James has brought Jane resurrection and salvation, even though she later denies it and then contradicts herself again. She is "ripped" by life and by the birth and we recall that Macduff, too, was "from his mother's womb untimely ripped." There are also puns in *The Waterfall*, as in *Macbeth*, on guilt, gilt and gild.

Ill-fitting and borrowed clothing is another recurrent image in *Macbeth*. Macbeth's clothes hang on him, says Angus, "Like a giant's robes/Upon a dwarfish thief." Jane

> felt herself to be nothing, nebulous, shadowy, unidentifiable. And yet she saw that this could not be so: that she was defined as clearly to these others as they to her, and that some of them might not flutter uneasily inside borrowed garments, as she did.

When they are first married, she and Malcolm avoid showy and spectacular clothes, "as though they might corrupt us" but later Malcolm becomes successful and takes to "camp" clothes, flowered shirts and so forth, whereas Jane has taken to dressing "deliberately, provocatively badly" in ragged old cardigans and laddered stockings. This is because she is afraid to be sexually attractive—her beauty seems to her "wild like an animal, that could not be let loose." Like Rosamund, she sees gifts like beauty, riches and intellect as potential sources of pain.

In temporary reaction against her experience with James, she thinks of the Hans Andersen story, *The Emperor's New Clothes*.

> the man is naked, like other men, and wanting like them nothing but what all men want. What were the things she had so admired in him, that had so moved her heart and touched her body? Nothingness, shadows, mockeries.

The thought of the emperor riding naked in procession, because he has been deceived, is here linked implicitly in Jane's mind, now she feels she has been deceived herself, with her memories of the naked James, wanting her, "wanting . . . what all men want." And the joy she found in his desire for her has melted all away, to her previous world of isolation and madness where nothing has substance. After the accident, she sees her love for him as having been "fatal, corrupt, a glorified irresponsibility."

In rejecting James (though only temporarily) she arrives at a grudging respect for Malcolm. We remember that Malcolm is perhaps the true hero of *Macbeth*.

Jane the poet thinks about literature a lot, appropriately

enough. Each literary allusion, though, is structural and used in a different way from the previous one.

> Comes the blind Fury, while I am in anguish, deciding whether to peel or scrape the potatoes, or whether to abandon them altogether in favour of some more convenient commodity like rice or macaroni.

This allusion to Milton's *Lycidas* ("Comes the blind Fury with the abhorred shears/And slits the thin spun life," says the poet, meditating on the brevity of life and the short time allowed for achievement in poetry) expresses Jane's preoccupation with death. We are reminded by it that she too is a poet (she measures achievement by the death of Keats), well read in the poets who preceded her. The conjunction of the philosophical and literary with mundane tasks characterises Jane in Margaret Drabble's usual skilful way as a married educated woman with whom all such women can identify, a fully realised individual woman in a recognisable, if extreme, situation. The conjunction is also a witty, and profound, statement by the author on the human condition. We are reminded of Rosamund and her income tax forms.

Margaret Drabble's educated women ponder the eternal questions of existence while getting on with their domestic tasks. Jane's thoughts turn at another point to Charlotte Brontë.

> Reader, I loved him: as Charlotte Brontë said. Which was Charlotte Brontë's man, the one she created and wept for and longed for, or a poor curate, that had her and killed her, her sexual measure, her sexual match?

This passage does several things. Jane, like the heroine of *Jane Eyre*, has the choice of two men, only one of whom offers her passion. Charlotte Brontë's division of herself into two, the real Charlotte and the heroine of *Jane Eyre*, reflects Jane Gray's own schizoid state and her preoccupations as a writer. Charlotte's death from pregnancy toxaemia after a few months of happy marriage confirms Jane's conviction that love brings with it fatality. And Jane is asking the question posed by her book, and which all artists must ask themselves: which is more important, art, the product of the imagination, creating a second reality, or life itself?

Like Charlotte Brontë, the heroine of *The Waterfall* dislikes

Jane Austen, but for different reasons. Her heart goes out to the "vulgarity" of the card parties at Meryton. It would be dangerous to conclude that Jane is speaking for Margaret Drabble. Jane's dislike of Miss Austen is due to the fine moral and social distinctions drawn in her books. Jane Gray objects to these because she was brought up in a household where such distinctions were habitually made. She fails to see that those she was brought up on were false, while those of Jane Austen have truth. Her hankering for the "vulgarity" condemned by Jane Austen is a violent, excessive reaction to her own miserably genteel background. She reflects spitefully:

> Emma got what she deserved, in marrying Mr Knightley. What can it have been like, in bed with Mr Knightley?

But there is no objective reason for assuming that the mature Mr Knightley would have made an unsatisfactory lover. Jane is distorting the book in the light of her own unhappy experience and provides it with an alternative conclusion which reflects merely her own needs: Emma "would have done better to steal Frank Churchill if she could," Frank Churchill, "lying and deceiving and proffering embarrassing extravagant gifts"—behaving just like James.

James reads Zola's *Therese Raquin*, a story of adulterous love and murder which ends in mutual hatred because of shared guilt; Jane reads Gide's *La Porte Etroite*. Translated as *Strait is the Gate*, the title reminds us both of Jane's physical frigidity and the Biblical reference, "strait is the gate and narrow is the way" to salvation. Salvation is what Jane seeks.

Jane's own situation is an explicit parallel to that of Maggie Tulliver in *The Mill on the Floss*, who also steals her cousin Lucy's man.

> Maggie Tulliver never slept with her man: she did all the damage there was to be done, to Lucy, to herself, to the two men who loved her, and then, like a woman of another age, she refrained. In this age, what is to be done? We drown in the first chapter.

By reworking the situation of a Victorian heroine, Margaret Drabble is once more testing the puritan morality which dictated renunciation. In modern society, the idea of "refraining" from

144

sexual experience is dismissed as ludicrous, but Jane finds that even though she does not renounce James as she has renounced the rest of life, a smaller, less dramatic renunciation is called for. James goes back to his wife, seeing Jane only occasionally.

When the crash occurs, Jane is filled with self-disgust. She is convinced the whole affair, "fast cars, vows, kisses, card tricks, the lot," were worthless. She has, in her own view at this moment, been judged and paid the price. But Jane's instinct for life re-asserts itself and she realises that James did bring her back to life. The affair continues, though Jane can arrive at no clear final estimate of its value.

The waterfall card trick is described by James as his *coup de grace*. The idiom he is in fact looking for is *pièce de résistance*. His skill with card tricks (associated with cheating, sleight of hand and card sharping, as well as the gamble Jane takes in accepting his love-making) is a parallel for his skill in making love. Left-handed, he calls his skill with cards "a sinister gift." A bar sinister in heraldry implies illegitimacy and their love is "illegitimate." Jane later describes her plea of imminent collapse as "illegitimate," though we see that both the love and the collapse were the real thing. Jane savours James's invocation of *coup de grace* as one of his "inappropriate verbal felicities." His lovemaking has brought Jane some kind of grace: his coming has unhardened her heart, and this softening is a prelude to her ambiguous salvation. But the dictionary meaning of *coup de grace* is a death blow or finishing stroke, bringing merciful death to the tortured. Sex and death are thus once more associated for Jane. The wages of sin is death, though Jane's belated sexual fulfilment brings not death, but judgement, in the form of a car crash which nearly kills James. A modern heroine does not die like Maggie Tulliver, but lives on in suffering and guilt.

Unity in this book is achieved partly by the network of inter-linked imagery, partly by structural parallels. Both Jane and James seem to have died, but both return to life. The bed, too, is an important symbol. In it Jane gives birth to new life, her baby Bianca, and in it she is brought back to life by James almost immediately afterwards. The bed is the setting for birth, copula-tion and death, central themes of the book.

Jane and James first sleep together immediately after Bianca's birth, so lovemaking is impossible. Bianca sleeps in the bed with them. Jane is forcibly reminded of her selfishness in taking James later on, when she shares a bed with his wife, Lucy, in the hotel, Laurie lying between them. Three-year-old Laurie is a more demanding responsibility than the baby, who coincides with (and is even an image of) Jane's regeneration, renewal, in the love affair with James. Lucy tells Jane how unhappy she is in her marriage to James, and Jane sees, disillusioned, that the "harmony of silence" between them is "largely weariness."

Every statement Jane makes is qualified, contradicted, or unconfirmed by the events of the narrative. She denies ever having been worried about her own identity. She claims to have had "vitality in excess," "unnaturally powerful passions"; but her previous descriptions of herself and of her state belie her.

Jane mentions the albatross which the ancient mariner in Coleridge's poem wears slung round his neck, a symbol of his guilt in killing it, several times. She admits that her picture of her love has been unreal:

> an unreal life, in limbo, without anxiety, guilt, corpses; no albatross, no sin, no weariness, no aching swollen untouchable breasts, no bleeding womb, but the pure flower of love itself, blossoming out of God knows what rottenness, out of decay, from dead men's lives, growing out of my dead belly like a tulip.

Love, like vegetation, grows necessarily for Jane out of decay: only God, she feels, can judge the extent of the rottenness, moral and physical, of the world. Here she demonstrates the puritan conviction that everything pertaining to the flesh is corrupt. She sees her own flesh as dead. This complex metaphor is characteristic of her state of mind. It shows her acute consciousness of the discomforts and strains of her own body, the fear that her lifeblood is dripping away, her preoccupation with death and corpses and her conviction that she herself is dead.

She sees rottenness everywhere: "I can't take, I can't give, because I know I'm such a rotten offering." James finds the bread has gone stale because she has forgotten to put the lid on the box. She feels it is immoral to impede the course of nature with a tin lid. If things are meant to go stale, she thinks, it cannot be right to stop them.

James retorts: "You're mad, my darling . . . you're like a boy who used to be at school with me who thought it was wicked to interrupt God's work by cutting his fingernails or hair, you can imagine what trouble it got him into."

And Jane is certainly mad, or on the edge of it. So uncomfortable in her body, at the time of the accident she feels as though her legs have been "severed at the knee by fright." James has told her stories of friends rising alive from their shattered cars, but instead of interpreting these tales hopefully, she chooses an image of fragmentation: they rise "as from a heap of shredded wheat."

Yet despite her conviction that she is half-dead, she is excessively conscious of her living physical body. Her nerves are on edge. She hears the needle "shriek" in the cloth as she sews. She hears the longed-for ring of the telephone in the "creaking cartilage of her own neck as she moved her head." In Jane's world nothing is clear or definite. Her prose rhythms express her dislocation. Many sentences are short, jerky, repetitive, without verbs; in other places the words tumble out after each other into long sentences in a spate. In no other book does Margaret Drabble use so many colons, or write with such violent rhythmic contrasts. The words chosen fulfil multiple functions. For instance, Jane the poet writes of "feminine endings." The dictionary definition is "an ending in which the line closes with an extra unaccented syllable in addition to the normal accented syllable." But the word also suggests the feminine destiny or fate, even death. Jane is possibly also thinking of her own pudenda: she is much preoccupied with "country matters." Thinking of James's skills, she reflects that there is "after all some skill in doing anything well, even an easy subdued woman." To "do" a woman in the vernacular means to have sexual intercourse with her. The usage is at least as old as Measure for Measure. Jane looks back over their "intercourse" where the word has both the social and sexual meanings. But in choosing the idiom "to do" she is once more casting herself in the role of passive victim, who merely suffers actions, instead of participating in mutual, reciprocal activity. She has accepted James joyfully, she was "easy," so here it seems Jane is lying to herself again.

Her difficulty in telling the truth comes from her all-pervading sense of guilt. She is terrified of her own sensations, her own emotions, which she feels are corrupt, and which she compares implicitly with blood: she fears the

> dangerous outward spread of emotion, a dark contaminating stain, which when undirected and unaccepted kills and destroys all around it, children, shopkeepers, parents, husbands, all . . .

So much preoccupied with liquidity, she has always hated the wetness incident to lovemaking. After her first experience with James, she is frightened. Even now, enjoying sex for the first time, her religious guilt at her pleasure expresses itself in terms of "destruction" and sacrifice. She suffers hallucinations of her body breaking apart on a high shelf, with everything falling away in the dark on all sides of her. Slowly she falls into James's arms, "quaking, drenched and drowned, down there at last in the water, not high in her lonely place." She is no longer dry and withered, like the plant she cherishes without much hope, but has taken her place, swimming with the current of life. Nevertheless, she remains afraid.

Later, after the disaster and some kind of adjustment, she says:

> I would flow in the course he had made for me: there was no way of returning to the old confines, the old high banks through which I used to run . . . the water I drank, the so much longed for water, was sweet, not sour and brackish to the taste.

When Bianca is born, when she "let her whole body weep and flow"

> she remembered from the first child the pleasure of that first bath. She did not know why they told one to put salt in the water; but they did tell one: and religiously she did, and would. It was healing, perhaps: all of her was for healing.

The symbolic potential of water is richly exploited in *The Waterfall*: water is made to represent life itself. It is necessary for drinking, for reviving animal and plant life, for cleansing, but one can also drown in it. Jane dreams of shipwreck, weeps "like a fountain."

Jane repeatedly uses the image of the current:

Since Freud, we guess dimly at our own passions, stripped of hope, abandoned forever to that relentless current. It gets us in the end, sticks, twigs, dry leaves . . .

Jane is thinking of the current which drowned Maggie Tulliver:

She drifted off down the river with him, abandoned herself to the water, but in the end she lost him. She let him go . . .

"If the current chose to rescue her, it could" she says early on, in her third-person narrative.

Rose, in her chosen isolation, her withdrawal from society, insists: "All alone, I arrest the course of nature. I arrest it. I divert the current." In doing so, she is denying the gifts of grace and riches which are hers. Simon tells her she is "very rash" and events prove him right. Later, he reflects that "her unassuming spirit" has brought her back to nature "by herself alone, guided by nothing but her own knowledge, against the current."

Clara feels her aspirations are "mad."

She felt she was breasting, rashly, the marching currents of humanity, and that she would in the end be forced to turn about.

Here the image is not of water, but of a travelling column of people. But whichever image she chooses, in Margaret Drabble's created world, it is always unwise to fight the current: one should go with it, follow one's instinct for life, hard though this must inevitably be.

Images of clothing and water are linked in the scene where Emma dives into the swollen river to rescue her daughter. Afterwards, she has to strip and puts on a mackintosh belonging to Sophy, from the theatre dressing-room.

Emma has already chosen Sophy, who, with all her deficiencies, is made to represent instinctive life, in contrast to Mary's virtues and limitations, and the gesture of taking over one of Sophy's garments in time of need seals the bargain.

After the discovery of David's affair with Sophy, Emma sees

there had been something factitious and self-willed in my praise . . . because I thought she was negligible and harmless, I had been prepared to see the best in her.

Like Jane Austen's Emma, Margaret Drabble's learns unpleasant truths about a relationship in which she had seen herself as dominant; she tries to be an escapist like Flaubert's Emma Bovary, but unlike Madame Bovary, she is not condemned to die: it is Emma Evans's destiny to survive.

The psychological and the symbolic are closely interwoven in Margaret Drabble's books. Rosamund, with the habit of integrity, unused to deceit, signs her maiden name in the register of the hotel where she is intending to share a room with a young man. (Though, in fact, he would have signed for them both, surely?) As Rosamund sees it, she forgot to lie for "some deeply rooted Freudian reason." But her forgetfulness signifies her obstinate virginity, which she keeps through the night, although she shares her man's bed, and her future status as an unmarried mother, who insists to midwives and doctors that she is "Miss," despite their concern to call all expectant mothers "Mrs." Rosamund remains spinsterish all her life, in spite of the baby.

Despite her shrinking consideration for others, Rosamund has a streak of hardness which shows in defence of her baby and, perhaps with less justification, in a withdrawn observant cruelty. Out to dinner with Roger she is amused to watch a fat American woman put ginger into her coffee instead of brown sugar.

> Fascinated, I watched her take a spoonful and stir it into her cup . . . she really gulped it down. I watched her face closely . . . she must have noticed, but she said nothing . . . she finished the cup. I have never made up my mind whether she was too drunk to know what she had done or had too bad a palate; or whether she knew quite well but wasn't going to admit her error.

This image shows us Rosamund's implied reflections on her own situation. Error (like *hamartia*) can mean merely a mistake, or a sin. Rosamund feels she has sinned, although she cannot decide quite what her sin has been. When people err, Rosamund is asking, is it through blind ignorance (drunkenness), a blunted conscience (too bad a palate) or is it that their pride forbids them to admit they have done wrong?

Rosamund feels her situation is a "judgement" on her. She and the American woman she feels so remote from have this in common: both act unwisely, but both accept the consequences.

Rosamund takes up jigsaw puzzles when she finds herself unable to concentrate on work later in her pregnancy. This is both surprising (because jigsaw puzzles are not intellectually demanding) and expressively characteristic of Rosamund. What, the author is asking, is Rosamund's research but a jigsaw puzzle, fitting bits into a pattern? Rosamund finds that as therapy it works extremely well:

> I found I could write my book and do a puzzle for alternate hours without getting unduly bored by either.

In Lydia's novel, Rosamund is accused of having a "jigsaw puzzle mind." The jigsaw is also an image of fragmentation. Rosamund is isolated, cannot relate to society.

Mundane objects and events take on layers of significance from their contexts. Jane Gray's struggles with the pushchair express the constant adjustment which has to be made to the obdurate facts of motherhood, and also Jane's peculiar difficulties with everyday tasks.

Imagery of heat and cold runs through *The Waterfall*. Jane and Lucy as girls are described as "cold fish." Jane repeatedly describes herself and Malcolm as "cold" people, and when all the heating in the house is brought up to the bedroom where Bianca is born, James (who thaws Jane out) enjoys the warmth. Jane finds the doctor's hands cold.

There is snow on the ground and the baby is named Bianca after this cold whiteness. Jane compares herself to a woman who gave birth alone in a hut in Alaska. The warm sun of Italy, where James takes Lucy and their children, is contrasted with the cold of Norway, where he plans to take Jane and her children.

As well as images of heat and cold, light imagery runs through Margaret Drabble's later work. Jane writes of her "own contradictory hallucinatory lights." She fears knowledge:

> it was so dangerous: how could one tell in advance, while still in ignorance, whether a thing could ever be unlearned or forgotten, or if, once known and named, it would invalidate by its significance the whole of one's former life, all of those years wiped out, convicted at one blow, retrospectively darkened by one sudden light?

"Convicted" brings in Jane's constant preoccupations with guilt and punishment, and the light image has its usual metaphorical and moral weight.

Light, perhaps more than any other image, has religious connotations: God said, "Let there be light," Christ is "the light of the world," religious sects seek "enlightenment" and "illumination."

At the end of *The Millstone*, George and Rosamund look down on their sleeping baby in her cot on Christmas Eve. Rosamund does not tell George he is Octavia's father.

> It was too late, much too late. It was no longer in me to feel for anyone what I felt for my child; compared with the perplexed fitful illuminations of George, Octavia shone there with a faint, constant and pearly brightness quite strong enough to eclipse any more garish future blaze. A bad investment, I knew, this affection, and one that would leave me in the dark and the cold in years to come; but then what warmer passion ever lasted longer than six months?

In this passage, light and warmth are combined. Rosamund considers that she has "seen the light" in her decision to keep Octavia and exclude the child's father. The mention of Octavia's "faint . . . pearly brightness" as an investment combines the puritan concern with thrift and the glories of heaven shining. The three of them, together on Christmas Eve, invite ironic comparison with the Holy Family. Rosamund is a virgin mother, emotionally if not physically. She still distrusts the language of the heart. Her own emotional capacity is only faint, and she distrusts the blaze of passion as garish and transient. Poor Rosamund.

The word "golden" is associated with light, sunshine, value and the glories of heaven. London and education together represent Clara's secularised heaven in an industrialised society, and all these associations are brought together in *Jerusalem the Golden*. Her image of her own heavenly city comes from a hymn Clara learns at school. In those days the words ran: "What social joys are there" though the line has now been amended to "What joys await us there." Clara also achieves her vision through the "light" of her intelligence.

The central image of radiance is strengthened by exploitation

of the possibilities of everyday language: Clara's school reports
are "predictably shining"; her mother at school had "shone and
prospered" before taking up her embittered anti-intellectual
stance.

When Mrs Maugham is dying Clara finds her early writings,
which include "O let us find a brighter world, where darkness
plays no part" and "Annabella, staring from her narrow attic
window, shivered and held her hands towards the solitary candle."
Clara's mother, too, had looked towards the light, but for her the
light had been quenched. The religious literature which Mrs
Maugham won as Sunday school prizes have "gilt-lettered" cloth-
bound boards.

Distance, however, can lend enchantment even to the grim
views which surround Clara in childhood: she knows from first-
hand experience the moral truth of a story about the

> house with golden windows, for she had once admired from a
> friend's house the whole, dazzling, distant smoky layout of her
> own hillside.

Clara's own name means "bright and clear" and she is herself
"bright" in the sense of having "considerable" intelligence. At
eighteen, raw from grammar school,

> she might not have recognised the Denhams' value, for at that
> age all people who were not from Northam seemed at first equally
> brilliant, surrounded by a confusing blur of bright indistinct
> charm . . .

When she finally gets to the Denhams' house, which for her
is heaven, she finds Gabriel's wife sitting on a long, well sprung
sofa,

> irradiated from behind by some small gold local source of light. . . .
> At the Maughams', all the light fell brightly in the small square
> bow-fronted room, from one central plastic-shaded bulb.

On her first arrival in the Denhams' drawing-room, somebody
is perched on a "gilt-framed armchair" and the room is full of
light,

> with mirrors . . . and chandeliers . . . and refracted angles of
> light . . . the eye could at first in no way assess its dimensions.

153

For Clara at this moment the room represents a heaven of limitless possibilities.

> Over the marble mantelpiece was a huge oval gold mirror, with an eagle adorning it and beneath it two gilt and delicate sprays of candle brackets . . . the wall that looked over the garden was not a wall but a window.

The Denham house gives a clear view of life at its richest, not a restricted and cramped privacy, as in the home Clara has come from. Clara here "sees the light" not in the old religious sense but the light of possibilities in life, what she has been looking for.

Earlier she has realised that there is room in the literary world for "fixed stars" other than Eliot and Graves.

In a complex image which concludes the book, we read

> She went upstairs to bed again, and she lay on the bed, looking forward . . . all the years of future tender intrigue, a tender blurred world where Clelia and Gabriel and she herself in shifting and ideal conjunctions met and drifted . . . like the constellations in the heavens: a bright and peopled world, thick with starry inhabitants, where there was no ending, no parting, but an eternal vast incessant rearrangement: and more close to her . . . the drive in the car . . . the wide road itself, the lanes of traffic, the headlights, the speed and the movement, the glassy institutions where they would eat eggs and chips, and put coins in the fruit machines . . . for the sake of amusement, and all the lights in the surrounding dark.

"Conjunction" is a favourite word with Margaret Drabble. It can mean fate or coincidence, a meeting, union or association, or the situation of heavenly bodies in the same longitude or the right ascension. All these meanings are present here. Clara has ascended into heaven. On her schoolgirl trip to Paris, she felt that the

> hillsides were crowded with the serried dwellings of the cramped and groaning multitudes, the ranks of the Unelect, and she the one white soul flew dangerously forth into some glorious and exclusive shining heaven.

She and Clelia and Gabriel meet "like the constellations in the heavens." A physical heaven is described, but a metaphysical one is implied. The world is "bright and peopled," "thick with starry inhabitants."* There is similarly ambiguity here: the stars in the sky are conflated in Clara's mind with her glamorous friends. Then Clara descends to the everyday world where she will be driven in a car (an image of sexual passion in Margaret Drabble's work, as we have seen). The "wide road" represents her journey through life and is contrasted with the narrow gate through which her "one white soul" flew out. She looks forward to the bright lights of the car, the all-night cafés, in the surrounding dark. She is going to amuse herself and take gambles with life.

Margaret Drabble in this book uses the imagery of light as suggestively as Thackeray does in *Vanity Fair*. Clara is a modern Becky Sharp, in that she uses her intelligence to climb into a wealthy family, where she creates disorder. She corrupts Gabriel's honour. But unlike Becky, she is not punished by discovery and expulsion. Becky ends with a life of pretence, calling herself "Lady Crawley": Clara looks forward to a life of deceit, concealing her relationship with Gabriel and "pretending to be free" of her grim origins. She has indeed found the "true brittle glitter of duplicity" to which she looked forward in childhood.

A Summer Birdcage opens with a meeting at Birmingham's New Street Station, and in the book we read that "churches and railway stations" are refuges of the rootless: rootlessness is the heroine's problem. *The Garrick Year* opens with an image of spontaneous enjoyment, with Sophy, David's mistress, eating chocolate cake on television, where Emma has wanted to be. *Jerusalem the Golden* opens with references to intelligence and luck, the two main themes. *The Waterfall* opens with an image of drowning, linked with images of fate and "the current." *The Needle's Eye*, a book about money and commercial society, opens in a shop.

Margaret Drabble, like George Eliot, is characteristically a novelist of intellectual analysis. Her articulate characters are endlessly introspective. They search their consciences and their hearts, puritan fashion, and make explicit statements about life and about themselves. But often their judgements are mistaken. As well as taking in explicit statements, we should look to the imagery, where the concrete objects and the plays on words are

---

* Clara's vision of heaven has more validity than the empty one imagined by Simon in *The Needle's Eye* (see Chapter 10).

integral to the created worlds of the books. Images are used to create atmosphere, to make thematic statements, to express character, to direct our responses and to imply moral judgements. As her work develops, the skill in handling images becomes an integral component of her creative art.

10

Landscapes, greenery, gardens

Un paysage quelconque est un état de l'âme.—Henri-Frederic Amiel.

Children are lost in such a land, where appearances bear no relationship to reality, a land of ha-has and fake one-dimensional uncrossable bridges and artificial unseasonable blooms: a landscape civilised out of its natural shape.—Jane Gray, *The Waterfall*.

Nature I loved, and next to nature, art.—Walter Savage Landor.

R. H. Tawney's metaphorical landscape in which the puritan dwells has considerable significance in relationship to those of Margaret Drabble. Having traced the separation of economics from religion after the Renaissance, in a chapter called "The triumph of the economic virtues," he describes a bleak world which Margaret Drabble's readers will recognise.

> . . . the puritan attunes his heart to the voice from Heaven by an immense effort of concentration and abnegation. To win all he renounces all. When earthly props have been cast down, the soul stands erect in the presence of God. Infinity is attained by a process of subtraction.
> To a vision thus absorbed in a single intense experience not only religious and ecclesiastical systems, but the entire world of human relations, the whole fabric of social institutions, witnessing in all the wealth of their idealism and their greed to the infinite creativeness of man, reveal themselves in a new and wintry light. The fire of the spirit burns brightly on the hearth; but through the windows of his soul, the puritan, unless a poet or a saint, looks on a landscape touched by no breath of spring. What he sees is

a forbidding and frost-bound wilderness, rolling its snow-clad leagues towards the grave—a wilderness to be subdued with aching limbs beneath solitary stars. Through it he must take his way, alone. No aid can avail him: no preacher, for only the elect can apprehend with the spirit the word of God; no church, for to the visible Church even reprobates belong; no sacraments, for sacraments are ordained to increase the glory of God, not to minister spiritual nourishment to man; hardly God himself, for Christ died for the elect, and it may well be that the majesty of the Creator is revealed by the eternal damnation of all but a remnant of the created.

There are obvious and immediate parallels with the world seen by Jane through the windows of her house where, although the electric fire burns brightly, her only view is of the snow-covered "brick desert" of London, as well as with her spiritual state. She is "cold," describes the distance between herself and Malcolm as "frozen wastes": she thinks of Alaska. She has practised "abnegation," and to win all, she has renounced all, like Tawney's puritan. She is preoccupied with winning and losing, gambling, profit and loss, bankruptcy, the moral balance of credit.

> Better to lose all than to be a capitalist of the emotions, looking down from one's guilt-constructed office tower on the hurrying throng below.

In this image, puritanism, renunciation, morality, economics and the modern city landscape are all associated. Jane's state of spiritual isolation and desolation, achieved by the "process of subtraction" bears a striking resemblance to the state Tawney describes. Jane has repudiated the Church of England in which she was reared, and doesn't "believe much in the sacrament of marriage." She is much preoccupied with election and fears she is one of the damned. She is not sure whether or not she believes in God: "My god is Necessity," she says.

Before Jane's marriage, she drives with James and Lucy (with James driving "too fast") to a pebbly beach where it is cold. Jane feels characteristically that her ankles are weak and ready to snap.

Landscapes in Margaret Drabble's books tend to bleakness: "bleak" is a recurrent word, and when views are described, which is rarely, they usually indicate industrial grime or pebbly beaches. There is never a golden, sandy playground anywhere: rather we find the "unplumbed, salt estranging sea" and it is usually cold. Her beaches are never crowded, merely occupied by a few lonely wanderers on chilly days.

Jane on the beach hears the water "sucking the pebbles from under my feet."

> What do you care for? said James, picking up one last smooth black round stone, circled with a pale eternal streak of whiteness. . . .
> "Nothing much," I said, smiling, turning away, gazing at the dead horizon.

Jane throws stones accurately at a post, which is possibly an image of her poetic gift. The metaphorical landscape she creates for us later, when James has brought her back to life, is very different:

> We were starving when we met, James and I, parched and starving: and we saw love as a miraged oasis, shivering on the dusty horizon with all the glamour of hallucination: blue water, green fronds and foliage breaking from the dry earth . . . perhaps, beyond them all, no ending but the illimitable, circular, inexhaustible sea.

The inexhaustibility of the sea, the discovered richness of life, contrasts with the bleak, dead horizons Jane saw on that cold pebbly seashore with James and Lucy before her marriage. The playground where James takes her and Laurie is different from the cold, muddy, grimy Greater London Council enclosure where she normally takes the child: this one is "high and open, with grass and no attendants." We are reminded of Blake's poem, "The garden of love."

Simon in *The Needle's Eye* walks with his daughter one Easter on a northern shore.

> The beach was a pebbly small bay, with caves and rocks projecting into the water, and large waves crashed threateningly.

In the same book, Rose looks out of the first class bar window on the boat home to meet her lover, now she is twenty-one and free to marry him; she sees the "sky a dull dove grey, and the sea had been a dull grey." Rose has been a ward of court.

> The court . . . would not have been much interested in the colour of the sky. Nor would Simon Camish, which is why she had not told him. This was justice.

Here the dullness of the sky represents Rose's dulled feelings: she and Christopher no longer desire each other when they are free to marry, though they in fact do get married. One of the themes of *The Needle's Eye*, as we shall see, is the conflict between love and law, between emotion and justice. Its main theme is community, and the problem of reconciling it with economic necessity, "the cash nexus." Rose lives in an industrial landscape.

> They . . . looked back at the view, where houses stretched, and tower blocks, and lakes of sewage gleaming to the sky, and gas works and railway lines, effluence and influence.

Here we have significant and thematic images of population, of industry, pollution, energy and communication, the landscape of industrial society, with its filth on the one hand, its power and potential on the other. They are linked to what Tawney calls

> the whole fabric of social institutions, witnessing in all the wealth of their idealism and their greed to the infinite creativeness of man.

Rose has tried to renounce the fabric of social institutions, to withdraw from society, but comes back to community to find hope in this very industrial landscape.

Simon has come from a grim northern town to live in London. He lived in Canal Street as a child, but his mother had spent her childhood at Violet Bank. Mrs Camish tells Simon (who is characteristically embarrassed, largely for prudish reasons) that from the outside lavatory of her childhood home

> you could see the birds. There was a kind of plant on top of the wall that you could see through a crack at the top of the door.

Even in the grimmest industrial setting, there are glimpses of nature. Simon, while at Oxford, visits the district his mother had come from.

Violet Bank, in fact, he later found, had not been named maliciously. It had once been a violet bank. . . .

Simon finds an old woman there who offers him a cup of tea and tells him

> she'd worked on the farm as a lass, but then she'd got restless . . . so she'd come to town and got herself a job in the chocolate factory . . . when Violet Bank wasn't built, oh it was lovely out this way, they used to come . . . on a weekend, picking flowers . . . oh yes times had changed, the farm where she had been born was all a big factory now . . . chemicals they made there, or some such thing.

This image neatly suggests the changes wrought by industrial development: chemicals, with their potential for good or ill, and used for artificial fertilisers, are manufactured where flowers used to grow. Looking at the "grim walls" and "dirty gutters," Simon has a sudden vision

> of the day when the world shall turn to grass once more, and the tender flowers will break and buckle the great paving stones. So recent they were, the days of green. Within living memory. And there would flow again the golden river, but there wouldn't be any people waiting for the boatman.
>
> They would have gone, the people. Hell is full of people, but paradise is empty, unpolluted, crystalline, golden, clear.

Simon's vision, though, is incomplete: what should heaven be for, if not for people? It is his bitterness, his lack of love for human-kind at this stage in his life, speaking in his vision of heaven as empty, in unpeopled purity.

In the grim industrial landscape where Rose lives, the great paving stones do not break and buckle, but greenery shoots through. Rose lives among what to Simon are only

> rows of identical houses, endless curving streets, the dark breath of urban uniformity, petty eccentricity and decay.

Walking with Rose, Simon thinks that she would not like her surroundings so much if she had seen what he has.

> And yet despite this, the walk did have charm: the buildings shone, gloriously washed by the heavy rain of the week before, plants were growing in the gutters. . . .

On a waste lot, a steep bombed site, they find a rotting, mouldy armchair: "grass and weeds grew out of its guts."

Simon's mother has told him

> one should never eat watercress that hadn't been cultured as it absorbed through its stems all the badness in the water—(what badness? what watercress flourished, lethally, on those Lethean canals on Teesside?)

In fact, uncultured watercress can carry liver-fluke. But Mrs Camish is showing her distrust of natural vegetation, because she lives in a grim industrialised environment. It is unlikely that watercress would grow naturally in the black, deathly canals, man-made as they are. At the end of the book, Simon has recovered some faith in life, and eats samphire gathered from the seashore by Rose's children.

Jane tells James that people have lost respect for the organic. Her metaphors are often vegetable ones: her friends are "normal people, real people with roots and branches, fed by the outer world"; her parents are "mad, dryly shaking their dry branches against the high gales of newspaper truth."

Lying in bed while snow lies on the ground after the birth of her second baby, she thinks of the contrast between "grimy brick-built London" and the Alps, where flowers are "trembling on those green slopes below the snowline." After her affair with James, she says

> I spoke of violence and convulsions but he made the new earth grow, he made it blossom. . . . He changed me forever and I am now what he made.

Growth, change, renewal and healing are all associated here with "blossom." Jane has a leafless twiggy plant on her windowsill. She has not thrown it out because it still possessed

> despite its barren decay, small faint green horseshoe scars on its brown stem that proved some hidden life—she did not water it. . . .

The plant is an image of Jane herself: she does not abandon life, although she makes little attempt to nourish herself: she eats baked beans out of the tin. She bears scars, physical and psychological, as the result of experience. But in the plant scars are a sign of hope. Later she drips a little water from a cup on to its dry earth. There is possibly a hint here of the communion cup, with its gift of eternal life. Jane wonders whether the gift will kill the plant with shock. Leaving home for the first time in months, Jane puts her plant out of the kitchen into the backyard, where "if it did not freeze it might flourish." Jane, who always speaks of herself as "cold," takes her chance, like the plant, in the world outside her home. She finds James "beautiful, like a tree, like a flower, like an angel." When James, in hospital, shows signs of life, Jane notices in her new rush basket "faint watery tender streaks of green." Earlier, vegetation symbolism had been used over-explicitly. "Perhaps people choose their symbols naturally," thinks Sarah. The aridity of Stephen and Louise is represented by dried grasses in long Swedish vases. Sarah's friend Gill always has vast masses of green leaves, chopped off trees or hedges, around her. Another friend, Simone, a gifted and original isolate, sends Sarah a black twig with one leafless austere yellow flower.

> Simone the flower without the foliage and Gill, the foliage without the flower. I should like to bear leaves and flowers and fruit, I should like the whole world, I should like, oh I should indeed.

Simone admires the *fin de siècle* poets, who glorified art at the expense of nature. Sarah admires Simone, but the prospect of such lonely freedom is against the current of her instincts, "the pulls of sex and blood and society." Sarah does not want to be another leafless flower. At university

> everything . . . is showered on one in garlands and blossoming armfuls until one faces the outside world.

Flowers for Sarah mean fulfilment, achievement and abundance.
Emma finds Sophy Brent "nice to have around, like flowers or a bowl of fruit": her legs are "lovely ripe extensions of her," there is "something wild and ripe that gives her away"; her skin has "a golden, full-bodied bloom, like fruit." Emma, finding enlightenment, reflects:

> Sophy Brent was in it by nature, she was on the side of all the flowering greenery, she was built for liaison and fruition, for passion, affection and infidelity . . . I had tried to pity her. I could not bear to think of my inferiority to such a girl.

163

Emma considers herself dry and spiky in comparison. Sophy is a bad actress because she is too natural: artifice is impossible for her. She represents (too schematically) the instinctive life Emma has been trying to thwart in her efforts to be smart and sophisticated, becoming absurdly and arbitrarily strict with herself. Sophy, seen eating chocolate cake on television at the opening of the book, represents pleasure. Putting on Sophy's coat after rescuing Flora from drowning, Emma recognises the necessity for spontaneous enjoyment, while accepting her responsibilities. She thus comes to terms with herself and with nature, or at any rate the novelist hopes the reconciliation is possible.

Since childhood, when Rose came under the "life-denying" influence of "grim, Evangelical" Noreen, she has made a collection of pressed flowers. They are a successful image of her instinctive nature, which she has similarly tried to crush and kill, to flatten out of shape, by adherence to Evangelical puritanism. Rose has been driven nearly mad by this distortion and her search for the London rocket, a "modest and unattractive" but "very rare" plant has been fruitless. Rose deludes herself that in her renunciation she has found spiritual peace, some fulfilment of her own nature.

But Rose is contradicted by the image. In pressing those flowers, in denying herself, she never found what she was looking for. Her instincts asserted themselves and took their revenge in making her choose the dirty, beautiful, flashy Christopher for a husband. Her choice of him is shown by the plot to have been a wise one. Here the imagery is used with effect and conviction.

Like Rose and Christopher, Nick and Diana come together again after a marital split. Simon thinks Nick and Diana "incapable of any real effort . . . as gracefully incapable as a climbing plant would be of growing erect alone." He thinks of a phrase from his bedside gardening book:

> It will not climb up on an artificial host.

He wonders whether Nick is an "artificial host," and of course, by a pun, he is.

Simon is "not a keen gardener; he tried to teach himself, from books, as he taught himself most things." But he has no natural aptitude and never knows whether he is uprooting flowers or weeds.

We remember that his education has involved "denial of nature" and "distortion of the will." His garden is paved mainly with "old stone." Simon the rock has a stony heart, as he very well knows. But every spring there are flowers on an old border and blossom on the trees. "Somebody had cared for it once." Simon notices that at his feet

> were the green shoots and grey flat spears of bulbs, and the foliage of such small-leaved plants as never perish, plants so modest that they never die.

There is constant life, and hope, to be found in the recurrent renewals of nature.

Living in Islington Emma and David have a garden which is all weeds, but the one next door "on the right" has been cherished by an old man through all the district's social rises and falls and rises again.

> His garden was a perpetual delight: the grass was mown and even, flowers grew at every season in every corner, and the walls were covered with every variety of climbing, blossoming plant.
>
> In the street in front of the houses there was nothing but dust and hard brick and cars and dirty children. One would never have guessed what secret foliage grew behind that stony frontage.

Accurate social observation is characteristically put to expressive purpose here. The old man has kept continuity with his roots, unlike David and Emma with their "classless chichi." In creating a beautiful garden in an area of brick, dirt and dust, he is making the best of nature. The image, though, lays the author open to a charge of sentimentality, of wilful primitivism. Emma and David, an actor and his wife, young in mid-twentieth century, cannot root themselves in one particular place. Is it even desirable—for themselves, for the author, for the reader, or in accordance with any sort of objective morality—that they should?

Margaret Drabble's greenery imagery is less successful on the whole than her manipulations of light, heat and cold or other more general symbols. The imagery of vegetation is at times used self-consciously, as in A *Summer Birdcage*; it is the least impressive component of the magnificent imagery of *The Waterfall*. At other times it is over-explicit, or inconsistent. In *Jerusalem the Golden* it betrays uncharacteristic confusion.

The "moderate leafiness" of the part of Northam where Clara lives "contributed to her hopes," though

> their own front garden consisted of a small oblong patch of mown but weedy grass, in the centre of which stood a small green flower-less shrub with dirty leaves.

This garden

> never looked impressive at the best of times, though in spring the daffodils would lend it a brief colour, all the plants were dirty, with the insidious industrial grime, and the evergreens were particularly filthy . . . the garden's sole glory was a laburnum, which blossomed wonderfully each year.

Both laburnums and daffodils are yellow, "golden" plants. But Clara has been warned of the poisonous pods of the laburnum, "dry, black and fatal." She has been taught to fear the consequences of anything pleasant and beautiful. So far, so good. The grass in Clara's garden is a small square, mown "grudgingly," and the herbaceous borders are "dutifully weeded." Mrs Maugham complains bitterly about the weeds rampaging in the neighbouring garden, and Clara sees it is true:

> One could not rot peacefully and harmlessly in such a neighbourhood: the airy seeds of debility would float too easily over the garden walls.

The grim, puritanical industrialised life of the north can tolerate neither weeds nor moral laxity, though the Maughams seem unable to keep the weeds off their lawn.

By contrast, the Denhams' garden seems limitless: it "seemed to have no walls, so thoroughly were its boundaries screened and disguised." But they too have weeds on the lawn, though they don't bother about them.

The house is full of plants and Clara likes this.

> She liked areas of doubt. Houses were not houses, gardens were not gardens, plants grew along picture rails, stone tables stood in the garden. . . .

Indoors, too, there is "a large pot of dying flowers." We recall that the house is a "lonely eminence" with an "air of tragic survival." In Clelia's room

> there was a plant, which grew and blossomed along the picture rail and climbed down a picture cord to embrace the frame of a small oil painting . . . there was the end of a brass bedstead, upon which other plants clambered and flowered.

Clelia flowers in these surroundings, like the plants, but like them has grown so closely into them that she cannot uproot herself and leave home. There are many "carefully arranged and ancient toys"; the room has "a sense of prolonged nursery associations." Clara does not see the possible drawbacks, only seeing in the "childhood objects," carefully arranged and lovely in themselves, a "link with some past and pleasantly remembered time . . . not violently shrugged off" as her own past has been.

Clelia says they don't go in for flowers in their garden: the Denhams don't understand them.

> "We can never remember their names. And we're too lazy to do any gardening. You don't have to bother with all this stuff, you just leave it, to grow weeds."

Instead of flowers, the Denhams have artefacts in the garden. They have a "dislocated" piece of mosaic, sculpture, urns and a "functionless fountain." Why is that fountain dry?

Mrs Denham's novel is called *Custom and Ceremony*, a quotation from Yeats's poem, "A Prayer for My Daughter." We recall that

> Custom's the name for the rich horn
> And custom for the spreading laurel tree.

The horn of plenty? The Denhams certainly live in material abundance. But there are no trees in their garden.

A possible answer to the puzzle of the dry fountain is that Margaret Drabble has in mind another Yeats poem, "Meditations in time of Civil War."

> Surely among a rich man's flowering lawns
> Amid the rustle of his planted hills,
> Life overflows without ambitious pains
> And rains down life until the basin spills . . .

"Ambitious pains" are just what the Denham children lack.
Yeats concludes that such a vision is

> Mere dreams, mere dreams! Yet Homer
>   had not sung
> Had he not found it certain beyond
>   dreams
> That out of life's own self-delight
>   had sprung
> The abounding glittering jet; though
>   now it seems
> As if some marvellous empty seashell
>   flung
> Out of the obscure dark of the rich
>   streams
> And not a fountain, were the symbol
>   which
> Shadows the inherited glory of the
>   rich.

The "inherited glory of the rich" is what the Denhams represent.
Richard Ellman interprets that "empty seashell" as meaning the
lovely emptiness of wealth. Moreover, a seashell, like a "functionless fountain," is a relic, dry and empty of what it once held. In
the poem, Yeats questions the "aristocratic principle" which for
Clara has been so triumphantly vindicated.

Writing about Coole Park, he is afraid that

> . . . maybe the great-grandson of the house
> For all its bronze and marble, 's but a mouse.

In the Denham household, as at Coole Park,

> Contemplation finds his ease
> And Childhood a delight for every sense

The Denham children are not "mice," but the only talented one
is Clelia, too closely tied to her home to fulfil herself. Annunciata
is still too young for her potential to be judged, but Amelia is
mad, Gabriel dissatisfied and Marcus, without talent, works
obsessively. The Denham parents have given their children "affectionate uncritical encouragement," which Gabriel feels "can't be
right." As Margaret Drabble clearly admires and respects the Den-

hams, it is surprising that she should give them weeds in their garden. Good gardening is clearly one of her positive symbolic values.

The answer to the puzzle may perhaps be found in Jane Gray's metaphorical childhood landscape, "civilised out of its natural shape." By putting art in the garden instead of flowers, the Denhams are neglecting nature, and this is the price of civilisation.

Yet, in another way, they represent, in their artistic opulence, unrestrained by grim puritan values, nature in its finest flowering. The problem is how to work with nature, so as to produce "leaves and flowers and fruit." Over-artifice, as Jane observes in *The Waterfall*, distorts and destroys. Nature, allowed to run riot, will produce weeds. Perhaps Margaret Drabble is saying that the healthy can tolerate a weed or two without too much anxiety. But the Denhams are over-civilised, not wild and uncultivated, so the imagery breaks down. This unresolved ambiguity diminishes the coherence of an otherwise impressive book.

Margaret Drabble's nature imagery is used, as we have seen, with varying degrees of success, but usually with overall coherence, as she wrestles with her essential moral problem: the conflict between instinct, represented in her books by natural vegetation, and the puritanical moral will, which causes so much damage to so many of her characters.

She remains ambivalent herself about puritanism, despite her intellectual wish to transcend it. This ambivalence is her weakness and her strength as a writer.

11

Community

Community! The joyful sound
That cheers the social band,
And spreads a holy zeal around
To dwell upon the land.

Community is labour bless'd,
Redemption from the fall;
The good of all by each possess'd,
The good of each by all.

Community doth wealth increase,
Extends the years of life,
Begins on earth the reign of peace
And ends the reign of strife.

Community does all possess
That can to man be given;
Community is happiness,
Community is heaven.

Owenite hymn.

To urge that the Christian life must be lived in a zealous discharge of private duties—how necessary! Yet how readily perverted to the suggestion that there are no vital social obligations beyond and above them.—R. H. Tawney.

Modern capitalism is absolutely irreligious, without internal union, without much public spirit.—Maynard Keynes.

There is no private life which has not been determined by a wider public life.—George Eliot.

Getting and spending we lay waste our powers.—Wordsworth.

Only connect.—E. M. Forster.

As well as examining the individual conscience and relationships within marriage and the family, Margaret Drabble sets her characters firmly in the economic community: all her characters have a clearly defined socio-economic status. In *The Needle's Eye* she explores the relations between men and money.

Buying and selling is an emblem of community in this, her sixth and most mature novel. In it the problems examined in previous books are brought together in an ambitious symbolic structure of a power and complexity which remind us of Dickens.

Its main theme is community, but in relation to it she considers the right use of wealth, "coursing like sap through the veins of England" (implicitly those veins are the roads and railways on the map), the demands of flesh and spirit (for man does not live by bread alone), capital and labour, law and love, the right relations between man and man in industrial society, communication between individuals and on a larger scale between different sections of society.

Although "we mortal millions live alone" each of us is bound to his neighbours by the ties of kinship and the cash nexus. Margaret Drabble's solution to the problem of isolation is for the individual to find harmony with his own nature in love. As in *The Waterfall*, she does not suggest that this solution is ever easy. Simon's bitterness is ameliorated by his discovery of the possibility of love, but his marriage remains intact and still unhappy; Rose finds that her dutiful commitment to love and community brings her no happiness, though it does bring about a revival of her courage.

As a social observer, Margaret Drabble is admirable: as a social thinker, she is less than original, although her view that love is the only hope for mankind embodies wisdom. She suggests no programme for social reform: Simon's rabid socialism is seen as destructive. Simon would like to do away with all privilege: Margaret Drabble is concerned with the right, constructive use of wealth, which she sees as a gift of God.

Political attitudes emerging from her work are left of centre, liberal and sympathetic to the underdog. Like Simon, she grieves for industrial workers at risk of being scalded by ladles of molten slag. She is no Marxist but it is probable that Margaret Drabble agrees with her Jane Gray that it would be wrong to become

> a capitalist of the emotions, looking out from one's guilt-constructed office tower on the hurrying throng below.

Selfish isolation, for Margaret Drabble, is always wrong: Jane and Rose only find restoration in returning to life in the community and sharing concern and love.

But before love and closeness can be established, there must be communication: lack of it intensifies personal and social problems. Communication is a major theme in *The Needle's Eye*. Communications between countries are represented by international trade, communications within them by railways and the telephone. In this book, too, there are significant difficulties created by language barriers between different nationalities.

Rose misunderstands when an old Greek woman points at the sky to signify that her husband has died. Rose smiles and says, yes, it is a nice day, isn't it. Africans are involved in misunderstandings in two centres of communication and community: the public library and the post office. The man in the library is looking for *Animal Farm*, and is told that the branch does not stock biology textbooks; Rose finds it, wrongly classified, among the children's books. The other African asks about a registered letter which has gone astray. The woman says she can do nothing till he can prove it has not been received. The African asks how can his family tell him they have not received his letter when they don't get his letters.

Rose reflects that so many misunderstandings are caused not merely by cultural differences, but by language problems.

Industrial society has provided one mechanical means of improved communication: the telephone. Simon, ringing Rose, is

> using her anxiety as an excuse for maintaining contact, much as one might use a financial debt or a forgotten briefcase or a family connexion.

This comparison draws together the main themes of *The Needle's Eye*: money, the law (there is a concealed pun on briefcase, as

Simon is a barrister), family ties, all in relation to communication. This example, like the use of the post office and the public library, is characteristic of Margaret Drabble's art. Commonplace concrete details are used to create a picture of our everyday, familiar world, and at the same time to unify her symbolic structures by amplification of her themes.

Jane, in *The Waterfall*, in bed with her baby in a snow-covered landscape, thinks: "I am better off than that woman . . . in Alaska, for I have at least a telephone."

The telephone remains Jane's lifeline, for though she cannot summon courage to go out of the house, she nearly always answers the telephone and makes occasional calls to the outside world. In desperation, she calls the Samaritans, and the kind man at the other end irritates her. She goes to bed wondering if he knows how futile his efforts have been, for she has not been able to reveal the true sources of her distress. Yet later she realises that the sound of his voice has consoled her.

> . . . he had probably never set himself up to understand, had never claimed to say the divine words of comfort, he had been content to play the holy humble role of service. . . .

The religious terminology is significant. By such unselfish caring communication, the isolation of the individual is mitigated.

Sarah in *A Summer Birdcage* consciously longs for "community." Like Emma, she goes to parties without feeling any connexion with the people there. She likes dancing with strangers in crowded spots.

At the end of the book she has not found a complete relation to the wider society, but her admiring love for her sister is at least recognised and perhaps returned, and Sarah finds some satisfaction in answering her sister's need. The first step towards connexion with the wider community is within the family.

Clara, in *Jerusalem the Golden*, seems to Gabriel everything that his wife is not:

> warm, enthusiastic, easily amused, amusing, and wonderfully, mercifully unexhausted.

Gabriel says, ". . . whatever may happen to us . . . you can never entirely escape me . . . nor I you, for you will never give up Clelia, so that makes us related for life, that makes you, as it were, one of the family."

Clara eventually becomes reconciled to Northam, and recognises this reconciliation of her two worlds by inviting Gabriel to her home. Recognising that her mother, who had "merely crushed and deformed what gifts she once had," once, too, had aspirations like her own, Clara

> wondered whether she should fall on her knees and thank Battersby Grammar School and the Welfare State and Gabriel Denham and the course of time . . .

Clara here recognises the need for gratitude to society and its institutions which have provided the means for her own escape. Previously her attitude, in her effort to escape and live, has been a limited individualism.

Gabriel is "on the whole an honourable man," but we get the measure of the way this honour is tarnished from his attraction to Clara's hardness. Clara cannot understand why Martin's wife should have been tugged back to him by her longing for their baby.

> For Gabriel the sight of so much indifference to the most tender points of his life filled him with a sense of liberation, of incipient gaiety . . . he thought of Clelia's enormous sympathies, of her arms more ready to receive the child than the man. . . .

Rosamund's arms, too, are more ready to receive the child than the man, but she has no "enormous sympathies." Theoretically a socialist like her parents, Rosamund considers herself concerned with social justice, but she exploits her privileges ruthlessly when it suits her. Until her pregnancy she has not really noticed how the under-privileged live. She has been careful not to go by mistake to Harley Street, where the thought of paying fifty guineas for what is hers by right would "outrage" her, "morally and financially." In the NHS waiting room she is shocked to see the poor, the decrepit and so many foreigners, anaemia and exhaustion in other pregnant women. She gets another shock after the birth when she is examined by five medical students, one after the other. Because she knows doctors must be trained, if they are to serve the community, she submits. She is nevertheless "outraged" that it should happen to her. She makes use of a family connexion with the specialist when she wants to visit Octavia in hospital.

Sarah worries about life's unfairness, but Louise disagrees. Louise says, "London wouldn't be London if it weren't for the provinces. Ox wouldn't have been Ox if it hadn't been for Redbrick. School wouldn't have been school if it hadn't been for secondary moderns. What can you do about it, except make sure that you come out on top every time?" Sarah says, "You're right, of course," but remains unconvinced. Louise later suffers for her selfishness. Jane, too, grieves over inequality, is morbidly guilt-ridden about "winning" life's gifts and its battles.

That life is unfair is the lesson Rosamund imbibed with her cornflakes. She is convinced that those who, like her parents, attempt to level it out are doomed to failure. Their reply to her childhood arguments was:

> Yes dear, nothing can be done about inequality of brains and beauty, but that's no reason why we shouldn't try to do something about economics, is it?

In deciding that her parents, from a "warm and fleshly" point of view, are as cruel as the father in *Washington Square*, Rosamund implicitly recognises that economics alone are not enough. But she remains unable to grow "warm and fleshly" herself. She is a prisoner of the "dreadful facts of life." In her relationship with Hamish

> I thought I was creating love and the terms of love in my own way . . . I did not know that a pattern forms before we are aware of it, and what we think we make becomes a rigid pattern making us.

After the baby is born, Rosamund learns for the first time to love, but she remains fundamentally inadequate. Her love for Octavia is tinged with selfishness, which she equates with maturity, and at the end Rosamund is incapable of sharing Octavia with George, of extending her love to anyone but Octavia. Despite her discovery, when she asks neighbours to keep an eye on the baby while she goes out, that if she asked more favours she would find people kinder, she does not mature enough to love her fellow men.

Her baby has brought her only partial salvation. Rosamund is still incapable of sexual love, a vital aspect of community, of commitment to others. It is possible, as we have seen, to read *The Millstone* on various levels, but far from displaying a mean female chauvinism and endorsing Rosamund's decision to rear an illegitimate child alone, Margaret Drabble is judging her. Ultimately poor Rosamund, so brilliantly created, so sympathetically analysed and understood, stands condemned. (Margaret Drabble takes the risk all novelists take in writing in the first person: imperceptive readers will take the character's views for those of the author. All four of her first-person narrators are individual creations, and all—except for Sarah—skilfully distanced. If we read closely, there is a gap between their understanding and ours, and this distance is a measure of the author's skill.) Despite her academic success and her courageous determination, Rosamund remains in "warm and fleshly" terms a pathetic failure, a severed head.

Jane's recovery is more complete: she discovers sexual love, which brings her out of isolation. Emma stops bothering about being frigid, and we guess her frigidity will disappear now she has recognised that she truly loves her husband.

When Lucy tells Jane that James will come to keep her company after Bianca is born, Jane replies, "I'd rather be alone."

Lucy retorts, "Who wouldn't? But alas, in birth, death, old age and infirmity, it's not possible." The physical facts of life make it necessary for us to call on one another for help. Jane sees herself and her husband Malcolm as "both exiles, both cold." In a neglected family she sees

> images of happiness: images of content. Fanny Price's Portsmouth squabbles. . . . Five children whose ages added up to thirty-seven. A man so tied to me that he cannot get away.

Jane imagines she would be happier under a yoke of necessity, looking with envious eyes at the underprivileged whose circumstances deny them choice, so they are forced to find a bond. Jane, unhappy and lonely, looks to the lives of others (doubtless as wretched as her own) for an image of the community she has renounced for herself, yet desperately longs for.

She finds such organic ties in her own family when her cousin Lucy rings just before Jane and James set out for Norway. The nexus here turns out to be economic as well as familial. Lucy tells her James is a fool to go to Norway when "we've been living on bread and cheese for weeks, and yet he thinks he can indulge in philanthropy towards cousins he's hardly ever set eyes on. . . ."

Lucy does not yet know that the object of James's irresponsible philanthropy is a cousin much nearer home. After the car crash, Jane takes three hundred pounds in cash from James's wallet and lives in an hotel. When Lucy comes up north, Jane has to lend her ten pounds of James's money as Lucy has run out.

This transaction, whereby Jane lends Lucy a tiny percentage of what is hers by right, confirms the ties of kinship and financial responsibility. Jane realises that she has robbed Lucy of her husband and of the financial support he should have given his family. (But just as she hasn't got the money to make full reparation to Lucy, having spent it, she doesn't make reparation, either, by fully giving up James to his wife. Margaret Drabble's later novels are unified into pattern and form by such implicit parallels.) Jane decides she must leave the Saracen's Head and her dream-world with it.

In the third person narrative her superego or conscience acknowledges that: "There was no question of keeping him: he had been lent to her, and the loan was over." Malcolm, though, who had "paid for her in cash and sorrow," "would pay for ever: he would never be able to buy them off." She remains married to Malcolm, but later reverts to "borrowing" James

Jane at one point doesn't think she could have slept with James in a house not technically hers: it would be dreadful to commit adultery on one's husband's money, "betraying both sexually and financially." Later, though, she decides that house ownership was "a mere straw of extenuation." Reverting to her characteristic mercantile-moral metaphors, she is not sure whether owning the house represents "credit or discredit."

Emma recognises that she and her French *au pair* have no sense of connexion: Emma is sure this is the result of the "economic nexus" that binds them.

> Not that I ignored her because I paid her, but on the contrary the fact that I was paying afflicted me so much that I did not care to intrude, by a look or a word, upon her privacy.

Only Mary Scott, among Emma's acquaintance, has the "social composure" to pay Pascale the right kind of attention, asking her questions about her home and family, her progress with English, bringing Pascale into her host community.

Domestic help is a thorny moral problem with Margaret Drabble's heroines: Rose is horrified at the thought of paying somebody else to do her dirty jobs. Jane and Rosamund, too, feel it is wrong, but eventually pressure of need forces them to conform to a social practice they feel is immoral.

Kirstin, *au pair* in Sarah's parents' home, daughter of a barrister in Stockholm, weeps constantly because she is lonely. Sarah sees in her an image of her own plight, that of middle class girls with no sense of vocation (nor consequently a relationship to the economic community).

Emma watches and wonders at the

> seemingly simultaneous and independent workings of so many bits of machinery that seemed to be me, and that seemed to make up, on a larger scale (all life being an emblem of all other life), society.

In recognising the emblematic unity of life, Emma is acknowledging the wholeness her consciousness of fragmentation intellectually denies. Her state of cold-hearted detachment, in which she sees the provinces as "curiosities," with a narrow social range for her detached "inspection," has within it seeds of better things. Even looking round Hereford and seeing a lack of connexion, she implies that some ought to exist:

> I was living in a small dissociated pocket of people who had settled in this town and who had no more connexion with it than with any other town in England. When autumn came they would move on. . . . And the town itself, which seemed to outsiders to be a unit, was made up of pockets of people, all as unrelated to each other as actors to farmers, or as farmers to teds in blue jeans. All that connected people was buying and selling.

The Needle's Eye opens in a shop, symbol of the economic community. Rose shops at the Co-op, the only surviving relic of Robert Owen's attempts to create a community at Lanark. Simon, shopping in a "mixed" area, is sharply reminded of his exile from his working class roots. He is critical of his friends, who choose to live in "raffish districts."

> NW1, this was, with all its smart contrasts . . . it appalled him, the complacency with which . . . friends would describe the advantages of living in a mixed area. As though they licensed seedy old ladies and black men to walk their streets, teaching their children of poverty and despair, as their pet hamsters and guinea pigs taught them of sex and death.

Characteristically incisive, this is powerful social criticism. Such frivolity, in its heartlessness, is equivalent to a form of exploitation.

Simon goes from the shop to a dinner party which, like that of the Veneerings in *Our Mutual Friend*, is a matter of surfaces, an image of false community.

His schoolfriend Nick and his wife Diana have previously separated but come together again, largely, Simon thinks, because they cannot survive outside their luxurious house. Their reconciliation foreshadows that of Rose and Christopher at the end. Rose and Christopher get divorced, the only couple in Margaret Drabble's books to do so: but they come together again. In her novels, love and community are the only possible sources of healing and renewal—divorce is no solution.

Simon looks round him:

> How rich they all were . . . where did it come from, this money, in this society that complained so often . . . of its ailing economy. . . ? By what strange turns had he come to be sitting there . . . with . . . wads of banknotes stuffed carelessly in his pocket?

A puritanical socialist lawyer, Simon considers it unjust that people who work in television should be able, just by being amusing, to earn incomes such as his father and Nick's had never dreamed of. Their wit is their only marketable commodity, and "what a price it fetched!" They imagine, thinks Simon grimly, that their wit can buy them off from judgement. Wit, the powers of intellect, are not enough for him without morality.

(Rosamund in *The Millstone* comes to a similar recognition: she had thought of "paying one's way" in terms of witty conversation and "a fine pair of legs." But she realises in adversity that these things

> were as nothing compared with the bonds that bind parent and child, husband and wife, child and aged parent, where money and responsibility are all that count.)

Money, responsibility and human ties are what *The Needle's Eye* is all about. Nick is what *Private Eye* calls a "pseud." At grammar school he emphasised the more affluent aspects of his home life and was silent about his working class maternal aunts.

> Then he had arrived at Oxford, sized the situation up . . . dropped his emancipated father and started to trade in his working class aunts . . . they were never, of course, allowed near the place: they worked better from afar.

The reader sympathises with this justified satire on opportunist heartlessness and pretence. Charmingly informal though they are, Nick and Diana keep the artificial *social* rules. Nick never wears a suit, but they would never allow an odd number at dinner.

Diana, like Simon, is "dissatisfied, uncontained." Simon dislikes his lack of ease with her, though he knows some people enjoy relationships which are "uneasy, tense" and "unfulfilled."

> But he, denied both peace and pleasure in lack of peace, was obliged to live in negation.

The word "negation" has here its full nineteenth-century weight. John Stuart Mill, in his *Autobiography*, writes of periods of

> criticism and negation, in which mankind lose their old convictions without acquiring new ones.

This is a fair description of Simon's state of mind. Mill is propounding a cyclic theory of history, in which periods of "negation" alternate with "organic" periods of growth and development. This theory of stagnation and renewal, stemming from the St Simonians, taken up by Carlyle and Dickens, is important in *The Needle's Eye*, as we shall see, on the levels of both character and national economic development.

Simon, driving Rose home and relieved that he is not expected to make a pass, reflects that it would be as hard for him to learn the codes of Victorian or Edwardian London as those apparently observed by Nick and Diana. He is puzzled by the mores of those he calls his friends, and can find no true relationship or community with them.

After her party, Diana is filled with panic: she feels such parties are all pointless, that she leads a stupid life. But she knows she'll give another one next week.

Simon's wife, Julie, gives parties which seem to Simon equally futile, and from which the children are excluded. Looking back to his working class grandparents, he admits:

> There were no virtues, moral or aesthetic, in tinned salmon or in hawking and spitting or in denying even the most minimal gleanings of a higher intellectual or social existence: but there was something hopelessly wrong with a life where a child sat in a kitchen eating a fried egg in terror, watched by a hostile alien, while adults in the drawing-room gulped down alcohol and displayed their unlovely hypocrisies.

The "hostile alien" is the foreign girl. Simon realises that he doesn't really know his three children at all. There is a split, too, between his family life and the work he does to maintain it: Julie dislikes having anything to do with lawyers, so he has to keep the two halves of his life apart. But he tolerates her:

> If people cannot accommodate to each other's prejudices, then what was the point of living together?

Yet another image of false community is provided by a charity concert to raise money for a home for disabled workmen. Looking at the affluent in their six-guinea seats, Simon reflects that "Come the Revolution" a few heads would roll. The wife of a "socially conscious" television commentator demonstrates her lack of real concern for the deprived and hungry by saying to Simon, "Have some nuts. I'm starving."

Even audience and performers fail to find community: a protest singer ("used to better from the gullible young") is badly received and flounces away; Rose, speaking from the platform, is completely inaudible, ineffectual, just as her grand gesture to Africa was a mere drop in that vast ocean of poverty.

New Towns, in this book, do not promise much in the way

181

of true community, either. A Labour MP, formerly a promoter of them, has become disillusioned with the "cheeseparing and commercialism" of the reality, so has almost lost hope.

Simon's mother, responsible for his rise and his consequent isolation, had formerly made attempts at community: she had "been a good socialist," had met his father at a WEA class, studying economics. But she scorns people who get into debt: her view of economics is still "pre-Keynesian." Simon considers she has the right to despise, having succeeded by her own efforts as a writer. He partly shares her economic views, anyway. But Mrs Camish's socialism was limited. Her vision of social justice implied only the creation of opportunities for advancement. She had wanted Simon to escape from the class into which he was born, but her vision had included no love, either offered or received.

Another minor character, Meyer, has no concept of community: in personal relations he is completely predatory and destructive, "with no notion that it was the slain that he fed upon" or that he was "doing other than fighting, still, for his life." No wonder Simon finds the social landscape, as well as the topographical one, bleak.

Although Rose finally sees that her withdrawal into penny-pinching meanness and isolation was useless because it "lacked community," she had been sustained by a vision of community experienced in her own village school, a world of "primal simplicity." She hopes her children will find it in their Victorian town school:

> in this brick desert, in this dense and monstrous urban wilderness. It had been a foolish hope, a ridiculous expectation, but it had been justified.

At the end of the book, despite Christopher's opposition, Rose wins her battle and keeps the children within the state educational system. She asks (unanswerably), ". . . what does the country have areas like this for, if they're too bad for children to go to school in?" Simon, the socialist, eventually sends his own boy to Bedales: "what could he do? The boy was . . . psychotic."

Simon's climb from poverty to riches is not unusual. Rose's desire to get rid of her money is, in his view, "singular, freakish."

182

Perhaps she is not the first to "nourish delusions of virtue." (Her full maiden name is Rose Vertue Bryanston.) Rose is convinced that the only right use of wealth is to give it away. But Noreen, who indoctrinated her with this sense of the wickedness of riches, could not have foreseen Rose's consequent legal troubles, "pale, in tears, confronting solicitor after solicitor."

Rose recalls herself sitting down

> with her dog-eared little cheque-book full of meagrely pared electricity payments, writing out with a shilling biro, Pay Akisoferi Nyoka twenty thousand pounds.

Nyoka built the school, but also treated himself to a white Mercedes. Rose's sacrifice is futile, but her motives show that her heart is in the right place: she chose to be interested in Ujuhudiana because it was a tiny place, with only one and a half million people.

"I thought . . . it would help me to understand what goes on on a larger scale . . ." but she discovers that "there isn't any parallel . . . between the building of a factory in Gbolo, and say the idea of building a factory in Anglesey."

With herself, Rose is absurdly mean: she tries to sew a new zip on a four-year-old purse; we see her "cutting up the rind of her cheese." As a girl she had a "massive allowance" and used to pay for everything when she went out with friends, "so they were always pleased to have me about." Such cupboard love is not true community, and Rose's abnegation is partly dictated by a search for a truer relationship to life.

Simon's wife, Julie, too, as a girl "could always pay the bill," so was welcome with the art school crowd she aspired to join. Julie in her thirties is "shiny with good health and lipstick driving *alone* in her big fat car" [my italics]. A typical consumer, her only real relationships are economic ones: with boutique owners ready to cater obsequiously to her acquisitive caprices.

> Brought up . . . in that vast building stockbroker's mansion, she had longed for the support of a terrace of elegant neighbours in an acceptable district of town. The Phillips could not have taken to the country proper, being townsfolk at heart, but they humbly acknowledged that they were now too grand and too rich to live in town itself, and had moved out, obeying the laws of nature, to a

spot where they could have their own quaking blue eyesore of a swimming bath and their own tennis court.

The words "humbly" and "nature" are here used with a biting irony. The humility which consists of conformity to the customs of a class into which one has climbed with a struggle is inevitably false, and far from the "penitent humility" with which, according to the Lutheran creed, grace could be won. "Nature" is used here with a backward glance at the naive eighteenth-century usage, when among other things the word could mean "what everybody else does."

Such acquisitiveness and ostentation, she is saying, is a hypocritical perversion of "nature." The Phillips are not using their wealth rightly.

Simon, in Rose's ancestral garden, has a memory of Oxford. Looking out then on a moonlit garden, where a mad old Fellow is wandering, he sees "some delusive allegory of the soul." But he protested then and he protests now "against the very shape of the trees themselves." He sees no point in "any virtue, any grace,* behind a gate marked Private." He prefers to let people trample the flowerbeds. Rose's rejections appeared to him

as the human, as the lovely, as the stuff of life itself.

Rose is here vindicated for Simon, but not necessarily for us, and we cannot take his political views as those of the author. The clue is that Simon protests against "the shape of the trees themselves": his own nature is distorted by his hard struggle, and he cannot see wealth or the beauty it buys without wishing to destroy.

Simon shows more wisdom when he tells Rose there is no getting rid of grace or riches. Rose's experience leads her to agree:

I'd always at the bottom of my heart believed that one couldn't get rid of money, that it would stick like a leech or a parasite and breed and breed and breed even if one tried to cut it out—and I was right, it was a real premonition. . . .

* Margaret Drabble here alludes to Walter Savage Landor's poem, "Rose Aylmer"; Rose Aylmer has "every virtue, every grace." This is a concealed clue to the interpretation of the spiritual state of Rose Vertue Vassiliou, who has grace without knowing it.

Even while living in Middle Road (the meeting point between Rose's wealth and her husband's poverty) Rose realises that

> no matter how energetically I get rid of whatever money comes my way, there's nothing to prevent my father leaving it to the children . . . they're his grandchildren, after all.

Even though Rose and her parents are estranged, the ties of kinship and inheritance are insoluble. After the reconciliation with Christopher, Simon sees Rose's next instalment of her fortune, the next thirty thousand pounds, hanging overhead like a "threat" of "death." He wonders

> . . . what will be the manner of your dying, do you hope to die in a state of grace?

But Simon is wrong. Rose's wealth is a gift of fortune (in both senses), and the right course would have been to use it in productive investment, creating wealth for others. Rose's husband, Christopher, is wiser. When he marries Rose, he goes into her father's business and does well at it. He cuts his hair, puts on weight, solidifies and "occupies space." He has become a "serious person."

Christopher goes on working for Rose's father after the divorce, although Rose's parents have cut off all communication with her. Christopher has an inherited talent for money-making, and one too for relationship, demonstrated by his attachments to Rose's parents and to the children. He recognises that the parable of the talents is partly about making money. The novel explores these and other implications of that parable. For Margaret Drabble, not to use what talent, grace, riches, intellect, beauty one may possess is a sin against nature, misguided and culpable.

Christopher turns the world of tax-deductible investments and proposed government policies for stimulating overseas investment (the real world, as Simon recognises) into

> a moonlight jungle . . . the balance of payments blossomed into beauty beneath his fingers. No wonder his father-in-law liked him. Who could help liking somebody so attached to one's own interests, so helpfully enthusiastic, so redeemingly involved?

Christopher's redemption comes from his involvement, in human relations and in trade which creates the wealth whereby we all live. Christopher, the bearer of the child on his shoulders (the significance of his name is spelt out in Simon's glimpse of a man carrying a child on the shore this way, whom he takes to be Christopher), is reconciled to Rose through his obstinate attachment to his children. Unlike Rose, he can reconcile love and money: she has foolishly tried to separate them, to get rid of her money and live on love alone. But her retreat into a poverty-ridden way of life had "lacked community" and was therefore invalid, a dishonest evasion.

Simon recalls that

> Rose had said to him once, speaking of her father, insensitivity beyond a certain point is sadism, and he had disagreed, thinking that people cannot help their natures: but perhaps she had been right. On the other hand, this man clearly needed people to talk to . . . about his financial affairs . . . and perhaps it was sadism in Rose, to refuse her participation? Rose thought there was a law above the human law, and that the indulgence of one's father was not a primal duty.

Here we have Rose's error "placed" for us: in putting her vision of God before mankind, she is guilty of a failure in human community, despite her desperate gesture of generous renunciation, which had proved so useless. Rose also finds out, eventually, the truth of "to him that hath shall be given."

Christopher is shown by events to have been right: he and Rose stay in their slummy house, but the district goes up in the world, is colonised by the middle classes, who even venture to follow Rose's example and send their children to the local state school. The property value of the house consequently rises.

Uhujudiana, the poverty-stricken desert of cracked mud where Rose's school was built, discovers its own sources of natural mineral wealth within its own soil. Previously, the war which burns down the school broke out when Urumbi wanted to secede from Nchikavu. The image is of a national community wishing to divide itself, like the amalgamated unions that Simon is professionally concerned with and who wish to be separated again, and the family life of Rose and Christopher when they were divorced.

The African country wished to split itself in two, and because the territory offered no economic possibilities for the developed countries, "no oil, nothing," nobody cared. But in the end, copper is discovered. Rose tells Simon

> They can't afford to mine the stuff themselves, they'll have to get South Africans and Chinese and Americans . . . in to do it for them, but they'd get the royalties at least, and there were people coming over already to study engineering.

Rose, so far from withdrawing from life at this point, thinks of visiting Uhujudiana herself. The book thus ends with a barren desert land finding within itself the natural resources for growth and renewal, and for relationship with the rest of the world in international trade. The productive skills of its people will be developed through contact with richer, more industrialised countries. Rose's gift, the school, was burned down, but the country can recover itself to a new period of organic growth. Christopher, not Noreen, had been right about the use of riches.

The business Christopher works in is owned by Rose's father, who had

> made a fortune in scrap metal, cranes, bulldozers, heavy plant of every sort: his company now had interests in building, contracting, property development all over Europe.

Mr Bryanston's money is devoted to construction and economic expansion, but the destructive potential of such development is hinted at by the mention of "bulldozers." His labour relations are "disastrous." Rose innocently gives a story about a strike to an underground magazine, so he asks her if she is a member of the Communist Party and cuts her allowance in half.

Simon, meeting him, is amazed at his attitudes: Mr Bryanston believes that the surgical equipment workers, asking for more pay, ought to be deprived, as a punishment for their selfishness, of medical attention for the rest of their lives.

> . . . Mr Bryanston gave himself away. He spoke of the workers as though he were a millowner in a nineteenth-century novel, even delivering himself of the classic view that the fact that he himself had started work collecting scrap metal in a handcart was a perfectly adequate reason why workers deserved no sympathy at all —a view which showed a mental leap so precarious, so ibex-like

from crest of unreason to unreason, that one could not but sit back and admire his magnificent, gravity-defying arrival.

Mr Bryanston has indeed a nineteenth-century view of business and society. As Noel Annan writes,

> Whereas in our time harmony in society is thought to depend on the economic structure, and reforms to improve society are measured by the amount they are supposed to improve the material welfare of the people, in Stephen's time the cure for social disorder rested in self-improvement.

Mr Bryanston has not advanced beyond the nineteenth century in his views. In giving him these outrageous (but by no means improbable) opinions, Margaret Drabble shows us the worst side of capitalism, its selfishness and brutality. This brutality is mitigated, though, by the wise influence of Mr Bryanston's son-in-law, Christopher, who uses his talent for money-making productively, creating more wealth. Christopher stands for redeeming love, which Margaret Drabble hopes can humanise industry. It is perhaps an omission in the book, though, that we are told nothing of Christopher's social or political attitudes, or his treatment of the men he employs.

The passage quoted from the novel serves a double dramatic purpose. It helps us to understand Rose's difficulties, stemming from such a detestable father, and marks Simon's progress towards charity: it takes a step forward as a result of his exposure to Mr Bryanston. Simon, until his illumination at the end of the book, imagines that "the right economic structure" will be enough to put right society's ills.

Having met Rose's father, Simon discovers a new sympathy with his own father-in-law, who at least retains some "fellow-feeling" for his victims and is therefore less corrupt. This is an important stage in Simon's development away from "negation."

Mr Phillips runs a mail-order business, which Julie and her middle class friends, cut off from the realities of life as lived by the majority, imagine is like the economical bulk buying they go in for, or postal systems run from boutiques. The mail order business is not illegal, but in Simon's "admittedly puritanical view" unethical:

Up and down the country unfortunate women were finding themselves obliged, to their amazement, to refund money for large expensive catalogues, and to make themselves responsible for the debts of their neighbours to whom they had acted as agents . . . a word which the majority of them could not conceivably have understood.

Simon feels his father-in-law's business is "stinkingly depending," quoting from *Measure for Measure*, where the business referred to is prostitution. Simon has prostituted himself in marrying Julie for her money. Elsewhere in the book, Margaret Drabble writes about the products of money as "effluence and influence," the muck inseparable from brass. As well as the lake of sewage in the industrial landscape (see Chapter 10) there is frequent mention of lavatories in *The Needle's Eye*, and of dust. Emily, thinking of Malthus, says people are like rats: "We'll start living in the sewers soon . . . the whole world's turning to dust." This connexion between dust and sewers recalls Dickens's dustheaps in *Our Mutual Friend*, sources of wealth, piled high with human excrement. Such a rich, almost submerged, pattern of imagery and allusion is characteristic of Margaret Drabble's narrative art in her fifth and sixth books.

Simon, having made the transition from the industrial north, where the men toil all night in factories, to the softer-living south, does not work with his hands, but sells his brainpower.

His father had received his near fatal injury while inspecting the safety mechanisms in the glass factory up in South Shields: he was telling the foreman that the women ought to wear hairnets at work when half a ton of machinery had dropped through the ceiling on to his head. It had been a famous victory, the women had worn hairnets thereafter. . . . Nothing would drop on Simon's head in Chambers, not even a dislodged cobweb, and nowadays young men were suing their employers for wrongful dismissal if told to get their hair cut for safety reasons. There was progress, certainly.

The irony here seems to be at Simon's expense: this is surely a limited and selfish view of progress. Simon has climbed out of his father's dangerous industrial *milieu*, but there are still ladles of molten slag and workmen who get killed by them.

Simon's present connexion with the industrial world is through his work in Trade Union law. Divisions and reconciliations into community are a staple theme of the book, and most of them show the participants having recourse to the law.

One of Simon's cases involves a man thrown out of his union for trying to form a breakaway group. The media start a "union hunt." Simon, representing the union, who want to get rid of the man, finds himself representing the management, who also want to throw out the rebel.

Simon "could not afford" (a quibble here) to lose the case. His friends say that the principle is doing an innocent man out of a job and that he is defending the "wrong cause for the right reason."

Simon's reply is, "That's right, that's how it is." The quibble on "right" points to Simon's legalistic morality. They are accurate in their accusations, he is saying, but he feels nevertheless justified, "right" in what he is doing.

> The union remained corrupt and Simon pocketed his fee. . . . He resolved never to work for the union again.

The muck inseparable from brass doesn't involve merely the physical kind.

Simon thinks:

> There could not be many precedents for Christopher's actions. He had perhaps created one. That was what happened, when eccentrics embarked on litigation. The law would tediously unravel, in accordance with its own concepts, the crazy acts of neurosis. He thought of other litigants, other madmen, passionately attached beyond all reason to cases they had no hope of winning: disputed wills, territorial struggles between embattled neighbours, angry wives suing long-defaulted husbands for shares in homes now given to newer mistresses. Such cases were never ruled by the mercenary instincts, though they seemed at the outset to be so: they sucked in money, sometimes every penny that the participant had, they sucked it into the mud of resentment and emotion, without a hope of final prosperity. There was a case currently being fought in his own field: two unions had amalgamated years back, were now struggling to disentangle themselves, to the obvious detriment of both.

The two unions, images of community based originally on ideas of brotherhood, wish to be divorced from each other, as Rose and Christopher have been.

> The judge had called both parties childish, and so they were, but they were past caring: they hated each other, they did not care if both perished, as long as the point was made.

Such hatred, says the author, is crazy, neurotic, and a waste of money ending in futility. The picture of such obstinate, senseless battles and their craziness reminds us of Jarndyce and Jarndyce, Miss Flyte and her birds. But just as Margaret Drabble's picture of the unions is juster and wiser than that Dickens shows us in *Hard Times*, she does not share his contempt for the processes of law as pictured in *Bleak House*. (The law in Dickens's time, it must be added, was corrupt and unreformed.) Simon speaks for the author when he says it isn't the law that is wrong, but the uses to which it is put. Her solution is the same as Dickens's: law can only be redeemed, humanised, by an infusion of the spirit, by human love and charity. The problem is that love is subject to law, though as Rose comments, quoting the Bible, the spirit blows where it listeth.

Rose begins to realise that the law and its processes,

> far from drawing lines and boundaries, are as self-perpetuating as the blows Christopher had given her during their marriage. They solved none of the confusions of the heart and the demands of the spirit, but instead generated their own course of new offences, new afflictions, new perversions.

When Rose first wants to marry Christopher, her horrified father makes her a ward of court, so she has to wilt abroad for eight months till she is twenty-one. Up to that time, Christopher and she have enjoyed each other in whatever "mud or gutter or dark corner or creaking second-hand bed" they can find. Rose's choice is "Noreen-inspired," indirectly, in reaction against Noreen's Evangelical influence because Rose sees in Christopher one of the "dispossessed, financially and racially," and because he is "sexy and undeniable and crude about it." But when Rose comes home and they marry, the passion between them is dead, a victim of the law.

191

After the divorce, Rose is bothered by letters from solicitors acting for Christopher, trying to get back the children. These are the letter, or letters, of the law.

Rose and Simon argue repeatedly about the letter and the spirit. Simon the lawyer sees value only in the letter: he believes that it is the spirit which kills and the letter only that gives life. Simon acts only from obligation. His sober Old Testament morality does not understand the "law's abridgement," the wisdom of cutting the ten commandments down to two ("love God and love thy neighbour").

Simon admits that he lacks charity and cannot love. Rose insists that in listening to her woes he has been charitable, "And charity is a form of love." Charity in the Bible means love, but Rose is thinking of the generosity which is one of the values endorsed in the book. Simon has both meanings in mind when he uses the word.

Simon insists there must be a "machinery" for public service. Rose says,

> If it weren't for people like you taking an interest in making the machinery work, there wouldn't be any. It's ridiculous to pretend that you don't care and that it would work all right if you didn't.

She is of course right: society needs people like Simon, responsible people who care for what is right. Rose sees that Simon is not so cold-hearted as he feels himself to be.

But he is right and she is wrong on other occasions. She feels guilty about bothering solicitors. She can never grasp that they have her interests at heart, but expects them to judge her. Simon points out that her problems are "their bread and butter."

Another time, she says:

> Interesting, isn't it, the things the law takes seriously, like bruises and adultery. It's a kind of code, I suppose, for what really goes on.

Simon says "one must have a code."

She is using the word to mean a kind of shorthand, while Simon means a set of rules. As with the quibble on the word "charity" the different interpretations they put on a single word illustrates their orientation, and their places within the structure of the book. Simon stands for the letter, Rose for the spirit: neither is adequate without the other, but they are doomed to stay apart. When Rose and Simon declare their mutual love, they also recognise that they are not free. In the wood where this declaration occurs, there is a fungus called "lawyer's wig" (the popular name for the shaggy ink cap fungus) growing from a heap of rotting leaves. Laws are necessary because human love is not strong enough to sustain virtue, without their support.

Codes on their own, though, are also inadequate without love and community to moderate their rigours. Rose sees her situation, persecuted by Christopher in pursuit of the children, as "a penalty, a judgement." She thinks of other divorced fathers who have remarried and hardly see their children again, without so "tormenting and dangerous a concern."

But Christopher feels that Rose had no right to divorce him, because "you can't make happiness out of destroying the lives of other people." Simon, talking to Christopher, perceives that it is the "underlying connexions . . . the truth he was after."

Simon tells him, "I doubt if the law will consider your activities express the right kind of interest."

Christopher's reply is: "That's because the law's got a bloody funny notion of human relations." And this is another key statement in this rich and complex book.

Christopher is, however, an unrealised characterisation. We never share his thoughts and he is only externally observed. He progresses from a seedy childhood, the son of crooked Greeks in Camden Town, to success in Mr Bryanston's business. Simon wonders how Rose could have married someone with the qualities she professes to despise: avarice, brutality, showiness, ambition.

But later he realises that Christopher is not interested in Rose's money, "only in power, and motivation, and emotion and love." It is Christopher's love, as well as his energy and his use of his natural gifts, that redeems him. Thus his place in the book's moral structure is shown to be justified. However, his character is submerged in the ideas he is made to embody, and consequently he never becomes "real" to us, as Simon, Julie and to a lesser extent Rose, do.

Simon, too, comes to recognise love, both in his feeling for

193

Rose and in a wider social context. His chief says, "It's no use asking Camish about it, he can't see the trees for the wood,"

> what he did precisely do was to see trees, not woods: he tackled each bit of life as it came up, he was a devoted believer in empiricism. . . . There was no way of putting the whole thing right, even if one knew what right was, in a capitalist society. . . .

In Margaret Drabble's picture of industrial society, there is no class of Tite Barnacles, as in *Little Dorrit*, "expressly born to set it right." She possibly sees hereditary privilege (which was dealt with in *Jerusalem the Golden* in connexion with the arts, not the world of business and administration) as irrelevant to political, as against social, power. This seems a limiting judgement on her perception, as political power is still, to some extent, inherited. The reader will agree or disagree, in the light of his own views, with her explicit rejection of political action as a solution. Hereditary privilege in the book is represented by Rose, who should have put her wealth into circulation, in accordance with the values of post-Keynesian capitalism, instead of trying to give it to the Third World in accordance with Jesus's teaching to "Sell all thou hast and give to the poor." Her husband Christopher manages to reconcile God and Mammon, through love. But we could do with a clearer spelling out as to exactly how he does it.

For Simon,

> . . . there was only the possibility of defending individual and minor points, redundancy payments, hours and compensations, laws of contract, conditions of work, rights to bargain. . . .

Simon has seen workers on strike the previous night on television, mumbling and shuffling (in implicit contrast to the glossy performers at Nick and Diana's). Simon thinks:

> The issue was of such simplicity. Those that have may not reject those that have not: they may not in any way accuse of greed those that have less than themselves: they may not talk of profits declining while still in their large houses: they may not sit in front of television sets in expensive hotels which cost one man's weekly wage per day and criticise men in overalls who do not understand why they should be laid off next week. . . . When

profits had so declined that owners too stand on street corners in their overalls and sell up their second car and their large house then they may complain. The naiveté of such a view was as bad as Rose's, ignoring as it did the demands of the nation and the economy . . . but it was fundamental . . . a view from which he could never train himself: it was the wood in which the trees grew. May the forests of it cover the earth, he oh so hopelessly desired. Shake down the superfluity. There was nothing else to hope for, any other hope was intolerable, and yet it was so hopeless it was as though one were to desire the kingdom of heaven. Where the rich may not enter, where Greed may perish. . . . Not of this world is the kingdom, but there is no other world. Oh God, he said, staring into his coffee-cup, a non-believer, Oh God, help us to help each other, for if we do not, what shall we become?

Simon's train of thought, about the trees and the wood, leads him to an echo from *Lear*:

> . . . Take physic pomp
> Expose thyself to feel what wretches feel
> That thou may'st shake the superflux to them
> And show the Heavens more just.
>
> (Act III, sc. 4)

Like Lear, Simon wants justice, but he does not believe in the "Heavens": "there is no other world" for Simon. But he comes, all the same, to the Christian conclusion, that the only hope is love, expressed in kindness. In *King Lear*, Gloucester also ponders the justice of the "Heavens," while doing an act of practical charity. Giving his purse to his disguised son Edgar, Gloucester talks of the "superfluous and lust-dieted man . . . that will not see/Because he does not feel . . ." (Act IV, sc. 1). Simon has learned, through loving Rose, to feel. Formerly he has acted from obligation, now he has arrived at conviction.

Like Rosamund's parents (see Chapter 4), Simon sees life, in Annan's phrase, "through the eyes of Mrs Webb." Margaret Drabble has a fuller, more complete vision. Annan describes life as seen through the eyes of the alternative, Mrs Woolf, as

> shapeless, often disheartening, although redeemed by beauty which appeared to give it meaning, though its meaning was inexpressible.

For Margaret Drabble, the world of Mrs Webb, of economics and hopes for social justice, can be reconciled with the "gleams of beauty" apprehended by Virginia Woolf into shape and wholeness through love. In one of her concrete, mundane but resonant images, Margaret Drabble asserts her belief in innocence and goodness in an image of commerce and community, a sweet shop:

> full of all the penny and halfpenny sweets—liquorice bootlaces, penny chews, gob stoppers, humbugs, toffee strips—that ignorant adults, who no longer frequent such shops believe in their arrogant adulthood to have vanished from the face of the earth. But the sweets are still there.

Checklist

of Margaret Drabble's novels and leading characters

A Summer Birdcage (1963)

Sarah, an Oxford graduate
Louise, her sister
Stephen, Louise's husband
John, Louise's lover

The Garrick Year (1964)

Emma, a housewife
David, her husband
Wyndham, her lover
Sophy, David's mistress

The Millstone (1965)

Rosamund, a research student
Octavia, her baby
Lydia and Joe, her friends
George, Octavia's father

Jerusalem the Golden (1967)

Clara, a university student
Mrs Maugham, her mother
Clelia, her friend
Gabriel, Clelia's brother

The Waterfall (1969)

Jane Gray, an Oxford graduate
Malcolm, her husband
Lucy, Jane's cousin
James, Lucy's husband

The Needle's Eye (1972)

Rose, an heiress
Christopher, her husband
Simon, a barrister
Julie, Simon's wife

Index